TY BUCKINGHAM

100% savings

THE STICKY AND SWEET OF FAITH, MONEY, AND PROSPERITY

GRAPE JELLY

Published by:
Oliver Royal Publishing
TyBuckingham.com

Printed in the United States of America.

Edited by Dr. Lori Wagner
Cover design by Bearded Creative Studio LTD.

International Standard Book Number: 979-8-218-19791-9

TO MY SON MOSES.
MAY YOU HAVE NO LACK.

GRAPE JELLY

CONTENTS

GRAPE JELLY

Introduction

For far too long I lived in poverty, not in regard to how much money I was holding, but rather how much money had a hold on me. No matter how much I would have, it never was enough, which actually sounds a lot like greed. Greed and poverty look almost exactly the same and are hard to distinguish on a surface level. In reality greed is a cover up for a poverty mentality. Greed is poverty with makeup on. It looks good. We even call it hustle. But these "never enough mentalities" didn't just hit my bank. My "never enough mentality" affected my soul, relationships, and how I think and believe.

It has been hard to find someone who doesn't have a little bit of poverty inside his or her soul. In so many ways we are born into a "poverty mentality". How do you know if you have a "poverty mentality?" A poverty mentality is most evident in how much people hate prosperity. Of course, we all want to do well, have enough money, and succeed in life. But the truth is, for most people, it doesn't seem to happen. The only thing harder than finding someone without poverty is finding someone with prosperity. This usually has to do not with luck or circumstance but with what we believe about ourselves and what we trust about God.

You are not destined to live a poverty-ridden life, not financially and not emotionally. I want something more for you.

If you answer yes to any of the following questions, you may be on track to have your life and view of God's provision changed forever.

1. Am I willing to address the parts of me that are holding me back from success?

2. Am I willing to let go of false beliefs that I may believe to be true?

3. Am I willing to believe that God wants something better for me?

I've found that **if I attach myself to the belief that I don't deserve more, I'm arguing myself into limitation.** When I think about my dreams and goals in life, I have to ask myself: do I believe that I can attain these dreams and goals? If not, can God help? The way I think about faith, money, and prosperity will determine if and how I achieve my aspirations. If I argue that prosperity isn't of God, I limit my hope for results. **When we deny God's ability and power to help us achieve our hopes and dreams, we are left with a God that we've constructed out of our own poverty. We deny God's gifts of abundance and prosperity.** *We deny God.*

PROSPERITY PREACHER

I know some people who hate what they would call "prosperity preachers." They are really talking about manipulators who say things like, *"If you give $100, God will bless you with $1,000."* This assertion is not only a selfish assumption, but it limits God.

I understand why people hate this. This limiting belief says that prosperity isn't good, real, or that God doesn't want the best for his people. Therefore, people are often trying to defend their lack. If they really believed that God could do what He says He can do, if streets really are golden for Him, if He really owns the cattle on a thousand hills, if He really does want to open up the floodgates of heaven so much that there isn't room to contain it, the lives of his people would be changed.

When people realize that they don't have prosperity, they often blame many things, while the main reason is that they've prevented it themselves. They push against it and anyone with it. This is why many people hate successful people, and while most successful people want to help those who struggle.

For far too long we've moved from receiving God's prosperity to only desiring His provision. If I'm honest, **I would rather preach prosperity than preach poverty.** It's better to preach prosperity than let others continue being in poverty.

WHAT THIS BOOK IS

Have people gotten faith, finances, and prosperity wrong in the past? Absolutely. However, I want to reclaim the idea of prosperity from a healthy way that leaves you wanting more from God, not less. When you believe what the Word says, it becomes a prosperous life to live.

> We've moved from receiving God's prosperity to only desiring His provision.

If you're wanting to go from poverty to prosperity, from lack to abundance to abundance, from fear to faith, you are holding in your hands a healthy and level-headed guide to help make it happen. This book will help you learn to drop your poverty mentality and the imposter syndrome we so often suffer from and regain the life you were meant to live. We'll look at getting rid of debt, how to create goals that lead to a more meaningful life and financial future, all while understanding that God wants what you want more than you even want it.

Grape Jelly

Each day when I got home from school, I'd start making myself a sandwich. I'd get two pieces of bread, avoiding the butts because I wasn't insane, grab the peanut butter, and then, out of the fridge I'd choose grape jelly. We had multiple jelly and jam options, but I always went with grape jelly. My stepmom Carrie saw what I was doing and acted as if she had just seen me yell at a puppy.

She let me know that we have more options besides grape jelly. Although for most of my entire life I had only ever had grape jelly with my PB&Js, I took a leap of faith, and I tried a different type of jam. Strawberry jam changed me.

From that day on, my stepmom and I have shared a long

running joke. We agreed that when we see someone, often each other, doing something that was "cheap" or "less than best," we would call it *grape jelly*. We would often say the phrase, "That's grape jelly," when we were really trying to say, "You deserve better than that!"

I think we've all had these kinds of glow up or grow up moments. Moving from grape jelly to strawberry jam changed me in a small yet real way.

Another memorable transition happened when I moved from my parents' house, blowing my nose with toilet paper, to having my own home, in which I placed tissue boxes in each room. If that isn't luxury, I don't know what is.

You may like grape jelly. You may be okay with it. I want to show you that there is still more out there. I still eat grape jelly from time to time, but what I really like is strawberry jam. Many of us have been born into families of origin and cultures, in which we are supposed to act as if grape jelly-type things are good enough for us. As long as we are okay, we are in good shape. But what if there were more options? What if God wants more for you than you want for yourself? If I can be so bold, let me suggest this: **God wants what you want even more than you want it.**

WHAT IS GRAPE JELLY?

Grape Jelly has become the synonym in our family for

having a poverty mentality. When you receive money, and you save all of it and don't spend anything more than absolute necessity out of fear, that's grape jelly. When you don't budget or think of the state of your finances, and you just spend without thinking, that's grape jelly. You deserve more than the fear that it will all go away or the lack of understanding to be a good steward with it. We have grape jelly mindsets that suggest that I either need to hide my money or spend it all. Deep down, we are afraid that we're going to lose it. Deep down we have a poverty mentality that says, "I don't deserve that." That kind of negative self-talk, that's Grape Jelly.

Grape Jelly believes you deserve less because you haven't yet had more.

WHERE MY GRAPE JELLY MINDSET STARTED

My grape jelly mindset started when I was a very small kid (okay honestly, I was a massive child, but you know what I mean). I remember watching TV one day in the afternoon of the summer, and a commercial came on for sneakers that had wheels in them. This was my salvation moment, or so I thought. My entire world changed. I was the perfect audience for this commercial. I loved to roller skate (I went to Christian skate night only as a kid, but still), and I also had to wear shoes. You could walk one moment, and the next you were skating. I still see these in adulthood from time to time. I thought they were the coolest things. Okay, I still think they're awesome, but that's neither here nor there.

GRAPE JELLY

I called out to my Mom, pleading with her to run to the TV, as I had no idea how much longer the commercial would last. She came in right at the end just at the moment when it broadcast the price and the phone number to call to order. I was so excited. They seemed so inexpensive. My family of origin didn't have a great excess of money for a variety of reasons, but in this moment, I thought we could afford this. The shoes were only $19.95! I remember telling my mom that I wanted them, and that I was so confident that we could afford them. Then my Mom told me the news. They weren't $19.95. They were 5 payments of $19.95, and we couldn't spend that kind of money on shoes.

Grape Jelly believes you deserve less because you haven't yet had more.

I was crushed, not because we couldn't afford the sneakers, but because, even though this wasn't said out loud, I felt as if I wasn't worth it. *As a side note this is a good reason, when you tell someone no, especially kids, to say, "We can't right now, but I would love that for you in the future when we can."*

This turned into years of asking permission for things I needed instead of asking a blessing for the things I wanted. I would ask permission to have a snack, to have fun, to do things that I knew I could do. I always wanted to make sure. This was the original grape jelly for me –getting only the basic things because I didn't believe I could get anything better.

Just to be clear, my parents never said this. These were lies that I convinced myself were truths based on little to no evidence. It took not just years, but decades to heal from this. I had an encounter in prayer that led me to heart healing, but I then had to have practical healing as well.

You could think, that's wild that I was so marked by one conversation over some wheeled shoes. But often times, the things that hurt us the most are things that we never dealt with as kids. Many of us discover as adults that we have hurts from when we were 5 or 6 that we have never taken the time to heal. Now we are 56, and we still react like a 6-year old.

I thought that this shoe moment was rough, but for me it got worse, almost comedically worse.

WHEN MY GRAPE JELLY PEAKED

I've only had one traditional job in my life. Only once have I had a job in which I clocked in, had a boss, and my taxes were taken out of each paycheck automatically. In high school I worked at a fast and casual dining place called YaYa's (You say you worked at fast and casual dining when you're too ashamed to call it fast food). After I went to college, for a total of 10 years, I worked for myself and did freelance graphic design for churches, nonprofits, and the occasional small business. I didn't mind it, and the money was good for a college student. However, after a decade of this, it seemed that every year my dream of being a full-time speaker and author was one more year away. **I was perpetually indoctrinating myself into a belief system that I was never going to have enough money to be able to do the thing I dreamed of doing.** Granted, a large majority of these thoughts were based on no evidence. They were simply broken parts of me that never healed as a kid.

Everything changed when I felt God speak to me in messages from my pastor, my prayers, and even dreams in the night. God was calling me to step out of my backup plan of graphic design and focus on what He had called me to do. I knew that I was being called to go into deeper waters and to have some wild faith.

I went to my wife and mentors and told them what I was feeling. Everyone was on board and was surprised I hadn't done this sooner. Here's where the grape jelly really peaked; I knew that God had spoken to me, yet from that moment on, I started begging God for the minimum amount of money I would need for my family to survive. I did the math on what it would take to have the least amount of money for us to make ends meet with my wife working full time.

$12,000.

$12,000 was the number I needed in order for us to make ends meet each year. I thought about the absolute minimum I needed, because I was often catastrophizing. Any idea of having more than the minimum that I needed felt unreasonable and impossible. I had a severe case of Grape Jelly.

I begged God for $12,000 a year. I would get on my hands and knees in my house and weep over the idea of trying to make $12,000 a year, it felt like a mountain of money. I was leaving my backup plan and safety net of graphic design. I was putting real faith in a real God who was calling me.

I had a date when I would leave graphic design and have no more clients who would pay me. Then I ended up getting a last-minute speaking event a week earlier than I had planned. I stepped out in faith with my insides trembling, because I didn't know if God was going to be there for me. I didn't fully believe that it was going to work out. I felt that there was no way I would make $12,000 in my first year of speaking to support my family. You know what's wild? I was right. God gifted so much more.

I was begging God for $12,000 a year. In my first month I brought in over $15,000. The rest of that year I ended up making over double what I did the year prior.

Not every month is like that. Not every part of my story is like that. What I have learned though is that many of us have *grape jelly* moments, moments in which we have radically less belief in our God, because **we tie our belief in God to our impoverished belief in ourselves.**

GRAPE JELLY

EXPIRED GRAPE JELLY

I believe that the single greatest way to expel and expire the Grape Jelly syndrome in your life, the way to break your poverty mentality and most of your money issues, is through generosity. Generosity is tied in with faith. It doesn't take faith to give someone $5. It may take some faith to give away $500. I want to constantly raise my level of generosity, because in turn my faith follows. Why? Because where your treasure is your heart will also be (Matthew 6:21). If you have heart issues, start giving away money, and you'll start loving where you send it.

Start giving away money, and you'll start loving where you send it.

"Well it must be nice for you to make so much money you can give it away," I hear you say. I feel it. I get it. But here is what I know: **I can afford to give away money by giving money away.** You can be out there holding onto all your seeds and then comparing your seeds to someone else's fruit. You will reap where you sow, but only if you actually sow.

The Bible says that God owns the cattle on a thousand hills, which is basically like saying God has all the money. (He has more than enough for you.) What I've learned to be true is this: if you decide not to be generous, and you don't give, you're going to be the one who needs giving the most. For me, I'd much rather be the one giving than the one who needs to be taking.

20

Reflection

WHAT AREA IN YOUR LIFE DO YOU MOST RELATE TO REGARDING THE IDEA OF GRAPE JELLY?

IF YOU COULD DISCARD YOUR GRAPE JELLY MINDSET, WHAT ABOUT YOUR LIFE WOULD CHANGE?

GRAPE JELLY

Your Money Story

I've seen the connection between how I think and how my thinking effects our money, both in what I do with it and how much of it that I have. Once I had a grasp of the content in this chapter, my finances realigned, my income increased, my conversations about money got healthier, and I had more business success. Simply put, this changed the money game for me.

You may not be aware of this but you're likely not just living out of how much you make. There's a good chance that you're living out of what others make too. When most people I know talk about their finances, they often bring up their families of origin, their coworkers who make more money, or even their future self. Most of us don't simply make financial decisions based on our income, but often on other's hypothetical incomes. We put ourselves in other people's money stories and make them our own, without any evidence that it's correct.

This may seem strange, but how much money others make might determine your life more than how much money you make. It's wild to me how many of us lived under our parents' roofs for 18 years, and then we continued to live as if we were still under that roof. We based our spending on what they made instead of what we made. If your family of origin had a lot of money, you might spend more than you have. If your family of origin didn't have money you might feel guilty for spending, or you might not spend, because of a kind of survivor's guilt, in which because you have more than your family, you feel badly about your abundance.

Often times, when a psychological event occurs, in which one person survives others they loved, the survivor of the trauma feels guilt instead of gratitude that he or she made it out alive. The survivor has an overwhelming feeling of guilt, and a "why did I make it and they didn't" attitude. Do you suffer from this? Do you struggle to spend because you grew up with nothing? Or do you struggle with self-worth because you have less than you were used to at an early age?

A season of financial struggle can be healthy, as it teaches you many lessons. However, it's not healthy to be perpetually in a money story that revolves around struggle. Your money story is the one that God has laid out for you. Here's a spoiler. It's better than you think.

I want to help you to see that we as human beings buy into various money stories. Many of these are stories we assume to be true, often without much or any evidence. These stories dictate how we spend, how much we save, and what we have.

The three money stories that can determine your life are these:

"Their" money story.
My money story.
God's money story.

"THEIR" MONEY STORY

The first story that we most often find ourselves within is *"their"* money story. That means anyone's but ours. We often make assumptions about someone's money story, which likely aren't true. We tend to tell ourselves stories about others based on a variety of things, but most often we do it based on our feelings rather than their reality. My example of this, a constant battle for me, is when I'm selling something, whether that be the speaking fees I charge or the books I sell (even this one). I've had books for sale for years. At events where I was speaking, I would always discount them. I would give a discount off the book, and then I'd add an additional discount if people bought two books. I was double discounting without anyone ever asking for it.

GRAPE JELLY

What's wild is that I've never had anyone complain about the price of my books (please don't start). People rarely even pay attention to the cost. They see the value I bring on stage and make the correct assumption that a book will simply be an added emphasis to the value that I've already given. Yet I would constantly give deals and sales without anyone asking. The only person I was affecting was myself, **I was making less money for no reason, except the fake reasons I gave myself.** I would put people into poverty without them ever telling me about their income or story. Which is pretty messed up honestly.

Here's another similar example. I speak at events for a large part of my income. However, I was constantly giving deals out before a person could even say I was too expensive. The story I would tell myself is that if I gave them a deal then they wouldn't be offended by my cost.

I would reject myself before being rejected by someone else. Being in *their money story* can feel generous, but what it truly is, is insecurity hiding behind fake generosity.

Who cares though? If people can't afford you, then maybe it's not the best earning situation for you. In my reality, I could charge what I charge because of value. If someone couldn't afford me, I could then afford to give discounts because of that higher cost.

When I stepped out of other people's money story, I realized how blessed my money story actually was. It helped me go from discounting before being asked to standing firm on my fee and often getting more than my fee. Once I understood that their money story didn't have to affect my money story, the story changed.

MY MONEY STORY

My money story for a while was contingent on *their story.* The story I would tell myself for as long as I can remember was, "My life is better is than theirs." It seemed better because I haven't had a boss since I was 18, I make decent money, and overall, I have more freedom than anyone I knew growing up, in college, or in the world. For a long time that was a good story. But one day, I had a coach show me that I needed to have a money mindset that wasn't connected to others. What if I could go from "my life is good because theirs isn't," to just having a good life? I started re-thinking in this way. Then I stumbled into something worse. I went from my money being contingent on their money story to my story becoming one of fear and lack.

My yesterdays' more than enough, became todays' never enough.

My money story has often been one of lack. My yesterdays' more than enough, became todays' never enough. When we first got married, we had no money, and if you had told me then what we make now, I would've

27

thought you were crazy. Not because it's *that much*, but because I had little belief that it would work out. Then on top of it what often happen is that we have one money story we tell ourselves: "If we only made X amount, then everything would be ok." Truthfully more money just magnifies what already is there, so more money rarely solves the problem. I know this because I make multiple times over what I made when I was first married, yet I can often act as if I still make less. I put a self-imposed inflation on my money by constantly devaluing it, even when it increased. Crazy right?

I battle a feeling of impending doom. *While today everything is amazing, I'm always worried that tomorrow is the day I will lose it all.* I have a coach who helped me see this. In my first session with her my largest thought issue was worrying about my speaking calendar being empty. It used to be the current year's calendar, then it would get filled. Problem solved right? Wrong. I would then worry about the next year, and when that started to fill up, I then would worry about years into the future. The Bible says not to worry about tomorrow; yet I took that and instead of worrying about tomorrow, I worried about 365 tomorrows from now.

Even in growth, prosperity, and stability, the higher the tower got, the more I feared what would happen if I fell off of it. In some ways, I had less of a grape jelly story for myself when I could only afford grape jelly. My money story is better than living in someone else's. My money story is owned and controlled by me and can be blessed.

But there's still a better story.

GOD'S MONEY STORY

God's money story for you is better than the story you tell yourself. God doesn't give out of insecurity. God doesn't feel bad about having you steward His resources. God wants what you want more than you want it. Yet so many of us do what I used to do: beg God for what He already wants to give us. I would do this by asking permission for what I already had ownership of --a blessed life.

> God's money story for you is better than the story you tell yourself.

I was praying one day, and God spoke to me as clearly as ever, "You're trying to convince yourself of what I've already communicated. You go to the budget, the bookings, and the bank for security. My blessing isn't tied to your security. I'm calling you out of other people's money stories, and out of your own. I want you in My money story. You can't budget for My blessing."

YOU CAN'T BUDGET GOD'S BLESSING

That line I felt from God hit me the absolute hardest. Because of "their" money story I would sabotage my money story by believing a lie about God's money story for me. I would look at every detail to convince God to bless me. I was trying to budget and make room for God to bless what He already wanted to give me.

God isn't asking you to refinance with Him. He just wants to pay for it. He is calling you to a place to taste and see, and He's told you that He's going to pay the bill for dinner. So many of us want to see the check even though we know God's paying for it.

We almost all start in "their" money story. When you get out of their money story and get into your own, you start understanding the weight of your money. When you get out of your money story and get into God's money story, that's when the whole world opens up. God's money won't make sense to "theirs" or yours. It's a story of sowing and reaping. It's a story of no lack. Some dream of owning gold. But in God's story, gold is His driveway.

God's money story has nothing to do with what you've made of yours or theirs. Even when you have a cursed money story for yourself, God has a blessed story for you. There is one main ingredient that unlocks the first level of blessing. It's called tithing, and it'll change everything for you.

Reflection

WHAT STORY DO YOU FIND YOURSELF MOST OFTEN LIVING INTO?

HAVE YOU EVER RECOGNIZED SOMEONE LIVING IN A MONEY STORY THAT ISN'T THEIR OWN? WHAT DID THAT LOOK LIKE?

GRAPE JELLY

Jesus Doesn't Need Your Money

Jesus doesn't need your money. He has so much of it that heaven uses gold in place of concrete, so I don't think He's hurting financially. The best part about tithing is that it's not about giving God anything that He needs but rather it's about **returning what is already His**. Part of this is worship, but most of it is a heart stance. It's a declaration that you trust God more with 90% of your income in His hands, than 100% of it in yours.

Tithe biblically translates to a tenth. This is why believers return the first 10% of gross income back to God through the local church. The local church is God's modern-day storehouse.

Jesus is the ultimate fiduciary. He has your best interests

in my mind when it comes to the health of your finances. The first thing I think of when it comes to Jesus talking about the health of our wealth is in the book of Mark which can be found in the twelfth chapter. People are giving. Many wealthy are giving large amounts. But Jesus takes notice of a woman who gives monetarily the least:

> *Truly, I say to you, this poor widow has put in more than all those who are contributing to the offering box. For they all contributed out of their abundance, but she out of her poverty has put in everything she had, all she had to live on.*

What does this mean for us? It means that Jesus cares more about the weight of the money than the amount of it. The amounts of course carry the weight of the smaller amounts; but the woman gave all she had, and it moved Jesus to say that she in fact gave more than anyone else.

So don't disqualify yourself out of healthy finances. You may be able to give more than people with more due to how you give. Jesus calls her a poor widow. Jesus knows her worth but calls out her value.

Jesus knows her worth but calls out her value.

This chapter is going to tackle the greatest subject in all of finances. No matter where you are at financially, you can step into obedience, and it will change things for you and your future generations. Generosity will change you. We'll get to that later. But tithing changes everything.

WHAT THE BIBLE SAYS

> *"Will a man rob God? Yet you have robbed Me! But you say, 'In what way have we robbed You?' In tithes and offerings. You are cursed with a curse, For you have robbed Me, Even this whole nation.* **Bring all the tithes** *into the storehouse, That there may be food in My house, And try Me now in this," Says the Lord of hosts, "If I will not open for you the windows of heaven And* **pour out for you such blessing That there will not be room enough to receive it.** *"And I will rebuke the devourer for your sakes, So that he will not destroy the fruit of your ground, Nor shall the vine fail to bear fruit for you in the field," Says the Lord of hosts; "And all nations will call you blessed, For you will be a delightful land," Says the Lord of hosts.*
> *Malachi 3:8-12*

There is no one on earth, either saint or sinner, who wouldn't want to put that verse, that statement, that truth to the test. The best part is that we absolutely can. To my knowledge it's the only time in the Bible where it says we can test God. In order to unlock that part of the scripture for our lives, we need to understand the fullness of what is going on.

This passage in the book of Malachi starts off with the question, "Would a man rob God?" (Mal 3:8), and the first thing I believe we all would say to ourselves is, of course not! Why would anyone in their right mind steal from God? The only reason people would steal from God is because they aren't in a right mind or just don't know that they are doing it. The passage continues by saying:

> Yet you have robbed Me! But you say, 'In what way have we robbed You?' In tithes and offerings. You are cursed with a curse, For you have robbed Me, Even this whole nation.

So, the premise is that of course you wouldn't intend to rob or steal from what belongs to God, but the Bible clearly shows us that when we don't give the tithe, we are stealing from God. Let's back up though before we go down the road of what happens when we don't adhere to tithing, and what happens when we do..

What happens when we tithe is that we enter into God's economy which is far different than the economy on earth that isn't run by God. Our earthly economy says you need to keep as much money as you can because it is yours. Heaven's economy, God's economy, says that none of the money belongs to you, and we are not owners of our money but rather we are stewards of His money. When we tithe, we step into a different kind of life, and that He will *open for you the windows of heaven and pour out for you such blessing that there will not be room enough to receive it.*

WHAT IS A TITHE?

When mentioned in the Bible, the tithe directly translates to a tenth of our gross increase and income and says that it should go to a storehouse, scripture's version of the modern-day local church that you are a part of. Tithing is a test of your faith. The Bible also says that where your treasure is, there your heart will be also. When you think about tithing don't think that this is something that the Church made up for God, but rather that God created for us.. When you tithe, you aren't giving, for you cannot give what doesn't belong to you. You can only return it. If you keep it, you're stealing it. Every bit of increase and income that we have comes from God (Exodus 19:5), so why would I steal from the one who gives me all that I have. It just wouldn't make any sense.

We need to tithe 10%, because when we don't obey with 10%, we are living in 100% disobedience. Jesus doesn't need your money. He just wants His money because when you do this you also give so much of your heart (Matt 6:21). What is so powerful about tithing is that tithing will do things that no budget can do.

WHY SOME PEOPLE DON'T TITHE

There are some people who think that they no longer need to tithe so they will argue that it's no longer for the modern church. However, what is the goal of trying to argue a tithe? Oh yeah right, because you're so much better with money, that you can do more with God's money than God can. What is the heart behind trying to get out of tithing? God sent his son Jesus to die for us, but we'd often die for 10% of what belongs to God. 100% belongs to God; yet He's asking us, testing us, loving us enough to command us that we give it back, so that God has our heart.

Tithe literally means a tenth. A percent is fair to everyone. It isn't like some political tax system where different people pay different amounts based on what they have. There is a fairness to it.

It's a test of our faith for sure, but it's also a test on God as well. Is God going to be faithful on His side of saying "I will pour out..." God wants to bless you, but it's dependent on us being obedient.

Many times, when I hear people argue tithing, H it's because they say it's under the law of the Old Testament. This is a strange point to make because the law, "do not murder" is also under the law, but we don't do that just because we are under grace now. Imagine I say that my wife and I got in a big fight, so because the law says you shall not murder and I'm now under grace, I can now murder my wife, that'd be insane, and you'd go to jail.

You don't have to tithe. You also don't have to be blessed. When you don't tithe, you're under a curse. Who wants that? **I can promise you that if you don't tithe, 90% of your financial problems will be tied to that 10% of your income.**

TITHING IN OLD AND NEW TESTAMENT

The most prolific passage when it comes to tithing is is the Malachi 3 passage which deals with the blessing of tithing while also addressing the massive downside of not doing so. Yet, that isn't even close to the first time it's mentioned. Genesis shows us that in verses 14:18-20.

> *Then Melchizedek king of Salem brought out bread and wine; he was the priest of God Most High. And he blessed him and said: "Blessed be Abram of God Most High, Possessor of heaven and earth; and blessed be God Most High, who has delivered your enemies into your hand."* **And he gave him a tithe of all.**

Genesis 14 Is a fascinating passage because it shows the idea of tithing happening approximately 500 years before the law was written about it. This helps us to have peace in that we don't have to worry about tithing being only an Old Testament law idea but rather a Biblical concept and principle that is rooted in scripture since the beginning of the Word.

Some people bring up that tithing isn't a New Testament concept, which is beyond wrong. Jesus himself talks about it in Matthew 23:23:

> *Woe to you, scribes and Pharisees, hypocrites!* **For you pay tithe** *of mint and anise and cumin and have neglected the weightier matters of the law: justice and mercy and faith.* **These you ought to have done,** *without leaving the others undone.*

The Bible deals with tithing in the New Testament. Not

only that, but it comes out of Jesus' mouth. Jesus is confronting the religious leaders at the time and noting that their tithing is right, but that they lack *weightier matters*. When Jesus says, *these you ought to have done*, this is a direct line saying that you ought to tithe.

Jesus says we should tithe. The greatest fiduciary that could ever exist tells you that it's what you should do. Jesus has our best interests in mind, and he wants us to tithe not so that the Church can have more money, but so that we can learn to trust Jesus' blessing and power over 90%.. Then we are in turn entrusted with even more. So often in my life, this has meant more money coming in, in somewhat bizarre and amazing ways. Other times it's God showing us how to stretch our dollar for greater gain.

"Yeah but the tithe isn't going to Go. It's going to a church where humans are." That is something I have heard before when dealing with the modern tithe. God doesn't literally need money, especially since it's really of no value other than that we say it has value. We only have value because God says we have it. The proof? Jesus died for you. You have so much value that Jesus paid (value) the price for your sin and all the past you've done, so you can have a future in the world and a future with God.

> "...Here mortal men receive tithes, but there he receives them, of whom it is witnessed that he lives." Yes the men manage it, but in heaven Jesus receives it.
> Hebrews 7:8

40

WHY DON'T WE SEE TITHING AS MUCH IN NEW TESTAMENT?

Jesus only talked about tithe a very limited amount... same with Paul. Why is this? Because it was common practice. The dentist probably isn't giving you a hard time for brushing your teeth. We all know to do that, but he or she may get on you for flossing. Tithing is like brushing. Giving is like flossing

Tithing is a biblical concept. The first tithe in the Old Testament was based on faithfulness. Then it turned into a command in the law. Jesus arrives on the scene and only talks about tithing one time. Jesus wasn't ignoring the topic. He understood that it was already common cultural understanding to tithe. Jesus didn't spend his time teaching on the tithe because people already knew to do so. Jesus taught on generosity to stretch their faith. Jesus was taking people to the next level. Now we argue about the first step.

LEFTOVERS

In regard to tithing, I adhere to the biblical concept of "first fruits." For "first fruits," you give the first and best 10% of your income to the Lord before you do anything else. I think of it like this. If Jesus was going to come and have dinner with you, wouldn't you feed him first? Wouldn't He get the first and freshest and best meal in the house? Of course, he would! Now imagine the opposite for a moment. Imagine Jesus comes to your house,

GRAPE JELLY

and you let Him know it's going to be a minute because you need to eat first and then you need to feed your friends and your dog. Then, if there is leftover of any kind, Jesus can have it.

Where your treasure is your heart will also be. That's why you do this first –to let your heart know what is first to you. When you get that paycheck, gift, bonus, or whatever financial increase, you give the first 10% to God through the local church that you're connected to.

GETTING TO GIVE

Tithing is the craziest blessing you'll ever be a part of. I was taught about tithing from a dad who didn't even live for Jesus at the time. When I was a little kid, my dad had great worth because of the boom of the internet and tech, but he wasn't serving Jesus at all. I remember though being a little kid in Bay City, Michigan when my dad told me about tithing. I was given money for something, maybe a birthday or allowance.

My dad told me that we need to tithe, because the first 10% of all we increase belongs to God. S,o we give it to the local church (storehouse), the one to which we are connected. In biblical times that storehouse would've had food in it, but now it has spiritual food in it that we consume. A healthy church should have money so that when people are hurting financially, the church can help out. The funny thing at this time was that usually I was the one asking to go to church. What my dad and I joke about lately is that even though my dad didn't fully know God at the time, he certainly wasn't going to steal His money. Even in a place of sin and lack of salvation, my dad was smart enough to know that you don't take from God.

My dad wanted me to live in blessing, not under a curse. He didn't raise me to be a thief.

JESUS DOESN'T WANT YOUR MONEY, BUT OTHERS ARE GLAD TO TAKE IT.

I wonder how fast you would leave your faith for finances. You may say that you wouldn't, but why did you take that job? Why did you move your family? Why did you buy that exact house? Most of us make financial choices that are thrilling demons. For too many people, faith comes at a price that is more expensive than the cost to leave it. Even Jesus was tempted by Satan with wealth in the desert. He offered Jesus all of the world if He would bow down and worship Satan.

I think about Judas. I love Judas, because he's most of us. He does all the same good, same miracles, same wonders, same accolades as the other 11. Yet he is only remembered for his wrongs. I wonder what would've happened to Judas if he had waited to end his life until after Jesus showed up, because I would be willing to bet you that Judas would've been the first person that Jesus would've gone to after He rose. I bet a lot more of us would our kids Judas because of the story of redemption. Judas traded his everything, lifestyle, relationships, and even his reputation for some money. This tells me something. **I can be close to Jesus and still be tempted to leave Him for some coins.**

WHAT HAPPENS WHEN YOU DON'T TITHE

If tithing isn't your standard, blessing won't be either. You'll live a life that's fine, but you'll be the one trying to make things happen. For many that may excite you, but in reality, if you don't tithe, you're struggling less with money than trust. Trust God with what He's entrusted you with.

> If tithing isn't your standard, blessing won't be either.

If you don't tithe, you won't be able to afford to tithe. You'll only be able to afford to tithe once you start tithing. It's weird math, but heaven's math is better than mine is every time.

Reflection

DO YOU TITHE? HOW'S THAT GOING FOR YOU?

WHAT DO YOU THINK WILL HAPPEN IN YOUR LIFE IF YOU NEVER STOP TITHING?

GRAPE JELLY

Money Goals

I once was on an award-winning soccer team. I don't bring it up a lot, because I don't want it to seem like I'm bragging. I remember being on the defense of some pretty crazy games. The games often ended with people rushing onto the field. Many times, the fans were so wild that they were kicked off the premises.

Technically I was in 2nd grade, and the award was a participation trophy. I never actually did anything, but I think that counts. I was on defense, and I wanted to be a goalie quite badly. I'm pretty sure that I was on defense that season because I was a really out of shape child and wasn't able to, as they put it, "run without passing out." The idea of my position was always to prevent any goals from happening. I swear that I never kicked that ball one time. Most of us little kids were just in the middle of field, trying to figure out the game.

Years later I wanted to make some extra money, so I thought it would be great to be a soccer referee for youth games. My best friend at the time did that and made some awesome money for being in high school. I got in the referee class, and after the first two minutes, I realized that this wasn't going to go well for me, because I knew literally nothing about soccer. I thought the class was going to teach soccer and how to ref a game, but I couldn't have been more wrong. At the end of the class, we had to take a test to become a FIFA recognized soccer referee for this local soccer club. So, I did what anyone in my situation would do. I cheated on the exam. I copied every answer from the person next to me. When he finished before me, I just guessed. I submitted the test to the front, and they never actually looked at it. They just traded it for the certificate and then a magazine of all the supplies I would need to buy in order to be a part of the team experience.

I never scored any goals, prevented any goals from being scored on us, nor did I ever referee any moments where anyone scored goals. Goals weren't really my thing, even if we all got trophies in the end (I still have mine).

Goals, however, are what will make budgeting, getting rid of consumer debt, giving, and investing worth it all. Outside of being financially healthy, this is how to become wealthy. **Money with plans is never as good as**

money with purpose. We all plan, which usually just means we hope that our money will go to the right places.

Before I had goals, I was never able to hold onto money. When we had that crazy moment in our lives where I had messed up our finances and ended up owing thousands in taxes more than I planned, this all happened because I didn't have goals for our money. We didn't have any real savings, investments, or anyplace where our money was planned to go. Our money was telling us where it was going. This might sound or feel familiar to you, because it's what most people experience with their money. This is also why so many people live paycheck to paycheck. My heart hurts when people feel that pressure. God never intended for you to live paycheck to paycheck. Once you start having goals, that will be a thing of the past. We need to tell our money where to go. Otherwise, we won't be going anywhere.

THE THREE GOALS YOU NEED

In regard to having goals, there are three main goals that you need in order to succeed with your finances. Having goals means putting faith into your finances, so that you can go the distance with it. You need three goals:

A GIVING GOAL
A FREE GOAL
AN END GOAL

GRAPE JELLY

You need a giving goal to determine what and where you will give. This goal often helps you to become a motivator and driving force for your free goal, so that you're free to give more.

You need a free goal to free you up in order to live a normal life without trading your time for money. A goal of being free from consumer debt, a goal that gets you free of paycheck to paycheck living.

Last, you need an end goal, a goal that puts your current finances to a future use for your future self and your future sustainability.

GIVING GOAL

When giving is the last thing on your mind, you give your worst not your best. My wife and I plan out each year how much we plan to give, and everyone gives differently based on their passion, purpose, and past. Our greatest area of giving takes place through our local church. We trust them to do greater things with our money, because it goes into a greater pot. When I give $100, that helps lives, but when a group of people give, it changes lives. We also have humanitarian giving, ministries, and then spontaneous giving. This is all outside of tithing. Tithing is the baseline, while anything over that 10% represents further giving.

You need to then plan how you give or you likely won't be prepared when a giving opportunity comes. There is nothing worse than having an investment opportunity and not being able to see the returns because you didn't have a goal to have that availability. The shift from thinking of giving your money away to investing your money in many ways radically shifts the heart.

Your giving goal will help determine your free goal, so that you are free to give. Once you're free to give, then you can plan for your end goal.

FREE GOAL

A free goal is a goal you have that frees you up to do what you want to do, not just what you need to do. Our free goal started when I looked and saw something awful. I got an account online that tracked both my credit score and the amount of debt that I had in certain places. When I looked at it, I saw that I had paid off 100% of a car loan and 7% of our mortgage, but it also said that I had paid off -0.82% of my student debt.

That didn't make any sense to me. If I'm honest, at first, I thought maybe I overpaid for a month. The reality was that my payment schedule for my student loan was so poorly managed that I had no real goal for getting out of student debt. I had made the longest payment schedule possible. I thought this was great initially because it made the payments as low as possible. Yet in three years of making "regular payments," it was actually costing me money to pay off my debt. I owed more than I started with. The interest was higher than the principle in my pay off schedule. That started a conversation of how we

51

GRAPE JELLY

can get out of debt.

You'll see a breakdown on this journey in the chapter, *Please Excuse My Dear Aunt Sallie*, but our goal wasn't just to be debt free. Our goal was to be financially free.

We paid off over $40,000 of student debt in a little over a year. That didn't complete the free goal. But it freed us up to have better free goals. Once the debt was paid off, our money then went to real estate and other future funds that could help us be free later on.

END GOALS

You may think this goal is figured out after you're free, and after you give, but I think this goal is the best one to plan out first. What do you want life to look like later in life? Then ask yourself, what would I have to do to get that kind of life sooner rather than later. **Your end goal should always determine your next goal.**

Your end goals shouldn't wait until the end of your life. How many people do you know who retire but aren't able to fulfill their dreams, because they didn't plan financially, physically, or mentally.

BONUS: MARRIAGE GOALS

If you're married or you have a goal to be married one day you need to read this section. **Goals made together are always better than goals dictated by one or the**

other partner. One of the greatest conversations you can have in marriage is the goal conversation. Ask your spouse what he or she wants to be free to do, where he or she wants to give, and what his or her end goal is. Each of these questions could be an entire date night in itself. Few things will make your spouse feel more heard than when you ask your spouse to speak about his or her goals.

Your goals don't need to be compromised because of each other. They get to be combined because of each other. The more goals you have, the more fun it can be.

"I WILL NEVER REACH MY GOALS"

Goals can often be daunting, if you haven't made a goal lately. A great way to make sure that you can make the goal is by creating standards for your goals. They need to have a heavenly purpose while also being possible during your time on this earth. Your goals need to be rooted in heaven but grounded in earth.

Your goals need to be rooted in heaven but grounded in earth.

The best goals are the ones that aren't made up by you, but are given to you by God, or at a minimum put before God. You want your goals rooted in a heavenly mentality, so that your goal has a bigger purpose than just the adrenaline and dopamine fix it gives you. At the same time, your goal needs to be

grounded in earthly context so that it's possible to complete. You have a goal of getting in shape. Awesome! But if you were to word the goal by saying you want to run a marathon tomorrow, you'd be a fool. Rooted in heaven, grounded on earth.

For my family that looks like having goals that are bigger than just our family but not out of this world or impossible to happen. For example, our free goal and end goals are quite similar. We want to be free enough to take risks and end up in a place where we have the option not to trade hours for money. Meanwhile our goal isn't to become a millionaire. That's arbitrary and hard to root on earth when it has no purpose outside of pride and a number. Let's be honest. If we hit our free goals and end goals, we often become the goal other people aspire to become.

If you think you will never reach your goal, re-look at your goal to see if they're rooted in heaven and grounded on earth. If they aren't both of those, set a new goal. The best time to make a goal is right after you've made a goal. Keep the momentum going. The person who wins the most is the the one with the most goals made.

GOALIE

If you're struggling to figure out the next financial step in your life, you need to go to your end goal and take the next step in that direction. This comes down to a much deeper question that we all need to pursue. What are you living for? What is your end goal? Biblically as a believer in Jesus, the end goal is to glorify God and enjoy Him forever. That's the macro goal for all believers. The intimate question is, what is your personal end goal in the pursuit of glorifying God.

What I love about this setup is that it turns our goals away from what we do for a living, and toward who we are for a lifetime. You are made for something better than grape jelly, the minimum. You were made for abundance. Do your financial goals match the goal God has for you?

Too often our goals are based on pursuits instead of passion. It may be in pursuit of being debt free or saving up for school. Or maybe it's all about retirement. If you're working in order that you can one day rest, you have the whole system backwards. Retirement shouldn't be to sit around. It should be to glorify God in a season of financial ability without restraint. Often times, I've seen people who are in pursuit of retirement. That's what they're dreaming of because they've never had a system of sabbath. You don't dream of resting if you have it built into your life.

You are the goalie of your goals. Defend your goals like your future life depends on it because it does.

Reflection

WHAT WAS YOUR MAIN MONEY GOAL RIGHT BEFORE READING THIS?

WHAT IS YOUR GIVING GOAL?

WHAT IS YOUR FREE GOAL?

WHAT IS YOUR END GOAL?

Saving is a Piece of Cake

I remember as a kid going over to my grandma's house for some sort of celebration. At the end of the meal, we had cake, because we live in America, and that's just what you do. Can I be honest? Whenever I offer someone cake for any reason and they say no, it gets under my skin. No diet or body is worth not having cake. So, my grandma was cutting the cake and adding ice cream to the plates of all the grandkids and parents. My plate came to me. It was just sitting there in front of me, looking at me, whispering sweet nothings into my soul. So, I did what any other kid would do. I ate the cake. For the record, it was a very small slice of cake, about the kind of slice you got at a wedding where you're almost more disappointed after you ate it because of how little there was to begin with.

GRAPE JELLY

So, there I was living my best life and yet looking for more. So I walked up to my grandma, as she was still serving cake to others. While holding out my plate, I asked for seconds. All of the sudden, as if in slow motion, as I say the last word of, "Please," to end my glorious quest of more cake, the entire room went silent. They looked at me as if I had just been caught in the deepest of sins. The quietness faded away, as the parents of the other grandkids begin to whisper to each other. I could feel their judgment, but I didn't know why. Was it because I was a larger than normal child at that point in my life? Or was it something much worse?

Apparently in this communistic household called grandma's house, there was an unspoken rule that everyone was supposed to wait to eat dessert until the host had started eating. That, for the record, felt like the most ridiculous rule on earth. I know what you may be thinking, "Well it's rude otherwise." Tell me this, what is more rude? To not wait before I eat the cake? Or to give a child cake and not let them eat it? This needs to be addressed. To this day, I don't really care who serves the cake. If someone gives me cake, I'm going to eat it, unless it's a wedding. Even so, I'm pretty sure that at my own wedding I was one of the last people to eat cake.

The best part about being an adult is that I can eat cake whenever I want. If I wake up at 2am and want cake, I can have it. If instead of having vegetables with my meal and I want cake, I can have it. If it's my birthday and I want to eat the entire cake and save none for anyone else, I would have no friends, but I could. Can I have cake whenever I want? Absolutely. Should I have cake whenever? Of course not. No one really would believe that in order to live a prosperous life that you should have cake every day of your life.

I think most people enjoy cake, especially when it is for their special occasion. Cake reminds me a lot of money. It's amazing and makes life better and the lives of others better. Even when the money/cake is for you, it should be for others too. When I have cake, I don't want cake alone. There is nothing more depressing than eating cake alone. When we have money, we enjoy sharing it with others when we can and when it's healthy to do so. We never give out of obligation, but always out of opportunity and obedience to what God may be telling us to do.

Let's say you have cake on the table. You know what you're going to do...eat cake. Now you might put it away, or even give it away when it's time for cake, but we shouldn't have cake always on the table, no matter how much we love it. This is why savings need to be put in accounts that aren't as easily accessible. Put the cake out of sight. If you don't, you'll gain unhealthy habits and run out of cake when it's actually time to have it. We used to have one bank, in which we had as many as seven separate savings accounts. The problem with

We never give out of obligation

that was that the money was always available for us, so we would use it. We would eat the cake because it was always on the table.

In the beginning of our marriage, I constantly took money out of our taxes account anytime I would go over budget, or just wanted to buy something that lay outside of our normal spending habits. One year I had done this way too many times. Our household that year lost a massive tax exemption due to employment changes. I send my taxes off to our accountant (most people will get more back/lower taxes when you use a professional compared to doing it on your own), and I am excited to hear how much money I get to keep after paying taxes. Since I have to pay my own taxes, I don't get a refund. I pay it all out of pocket instead of out of a paycheck like many households. When you get money back from your taxes, you basically have just given the government an interest-free loan for an entire year - something they will never do for you. So, when you get money back on your taxes, it's not time to buy a boat. It's time to put it away somewhere healthy.

I got a call from my accountant at the time, and she was worried for me. I asked her how much I owed (because I always owed taxes since I had to save my own). She told me that we owed $5,000 more than I had saved. This was not my best day.

Luckily, we had some savings, although not enough to cover all of that, so for the next couple months, we had to

hustle to get extra income outside of our normal budget-
ed income. We did. After a lot of hustle and a lot of not
buying anything outside of needs, we were able to move
on and not die of starvation. Something had to change. I
had this figurative cake so accessible on my table in my
one bank account that I would eat it all the time. I was
eating so much of our savings cake that it was becoming
an unhealthy financial environment.

We met with someone, and that person changed the
game for us. Asking for help with your money is sometimes the best thing you can do. A simple rule of thumb
is to have someone help you with money who you know
is better at money. We met with our mentors, and they
gave us great wisdom that I want to pass on. It's changed
our lives.

The advice is this: don't have your cake on the table.

Maybe they say it like that, but that's the advice I want
to give to you. Now when we are talking about cake,
it's mainly your emergency fund which for us is multiple months of expenses. Start with anything, since the
majority of people living in the United States don't have
access to even $1,000 if they needed it.

What we did and what we encourage people to do is to
open up a fee-free savings account at a reputable bank
or establishment where you can link transfers between
your banks. The goal is for it to be obtainable but not
easily accessible. If the idea of that scares you, remember

that with most of these banks you can just go to the bank and get the money if you need it. But to transfer it, it will usually take a couple of days. That buffer helps you decide if this really is an emergency or savings worthy. We now have multiple accounts, but some of them aren't able to be transferred right away. It takes 3 days to transfer. We are keeping the cake away from the table.

This can be used to save for vacation, a car, or really anything that you're trying to set as a financial goal. You will never reach a financial goal if the finances are easily within reach. It's human nature that when we feel like having something, we buy it.

If there is cake, I eat cake, because I love cake. I love money. For whatever reason, in the faith, we are not supposed to say, that because it may mean something we do not mean. But I love money and what it does for me, my house, and the people around me. Money changes everything, because anything that you are believing God to do in the kingdom is going to cost money. **The worst thing that can happen is that God wants you to have some cake with some friends, but you ended up eating it all before the party.**

There are three places you can put your cake. On the table, in the fridge, or in the freezer. Where is yours?

FREEZER CAKE
My wife Rebecca and I took part in a popular tradition.. For our wedding, we had one of the best designed and

even better tasting cakes that I have ever had. Our bakery made a duplicate of the top of the cake for us to freeze. We got home from the wedding, and one of the first things we did was to put that cake in the freezer. It wasn't the first thing we did, but you get it.

A year later we were thrilled to be celebrating our first anniversary in our small one-bedroom apartment. We got the cake out of the freezer. As we started unwrapping the cake from its foil, we were getting more and more excited. Our cake was a key lime and orange velvet cake. Oh how I missed it. We got the massive piece of cake out, we each ran to the utensil drawer, grabbed a fork and then rushed to see who would get the first bite. We felt like we had just won the best prize for surviving a year of marriage. We both stabbed the cake at the same time, but we didn't eat it. It wasn't because we didn't want to, but rather because we couldn't. In all the excitement, we had forgotten a key part of this cake. It had been frozen for a year, and it hadn't thawed out in the 30 seconds we had it out.

We had all the excitement and celebration ready, yet our cake was impossible to eat. Certain savings accounts and structures for savings are like this. Long-term savings can be difficult, costly, or impossible to get within a day's notice. This isn't an ideal place for your savings until you also have some accessible savings. We have a variety of savings structures that are similar to this that would take up to a week or so to get access to. There are many benefits of this kind of savings account, as it is

GRAPE JELLY

growing more than others; however, it isn't really meant to be used. It's like a special cake, reserved only for a once a year taste if you will.

TABLE CAKE

Table cake is only meant for specific moments. However, everyone should have some amount of money, at least a few hundred dollars accessible in case of unexpected expenses each month. Minor unexpected purchases need easy access to funds.

FRIDGE CAKE

Many scholars have debated in great lengths about where you should store your birthday cake. Some believe that on the table, under a glass protector is best. You view it and can eat it instantly. Others, like myself, believe that cake belongs in the fridge. I personally want almost everything sweet in a fridge, even candy bars.

For most, this is the best place to have your savings. A place that takes just a few days to get hold of. Medium purchases need to have some space, so that it slows you down to make sure you are making the right purchase at the right time.

FREEZER CAKE: Long term savings only to be taken out in major emergencies or life events. *These are often CDs (certificate of deposits), high cash value whole life policies, or retirement accounts.*

FRIDGE CAKE: The majority of savings you allocate should be here. It slows you down and forces you to think about it over a couple of days. *These are going to be savings accounts, often at a bank separate from your checking account. These often take two to three days to access funds.*

TABLE CAKE: You need to have access to extra funds outside of your normal monthly budget in case of unexpected expenses that almost always come up in any month. *This is your typical savings account that you can access instantly, or the cash you have hidden in your piggy bank.*

At the end of the day, there's no right or wrong place to have cake. Cake is amazing. **The issue isn't as much where it's located as the discipline you have with where it's located.** Maybe you can handle all of your money being in duffle bag on your counter. I know I couldn't.

What this does is it makes us ask more important questions when we spend. How you save will determine how you spend. What would it look like if your money wasn't always instantly accessible? If you had separate funds and places where most of it was in the freezer, some of it was in the fridge, and only a little bit was instantly accessible, how would that make you feel? What it should make you feel is that you're moving too fast with your buying if you always need to see your cake on the table. If your spending is in a healthy place, there should be no need for all your cake to be on the table. That's how people get into unhealthy places.

Reflection

HOW MUCH CAKE ARE YOU EATING? IS YOUR SAVINGS ALL IN ONE PLACE OR IS IT DIVERSIFIED?

HOW MUCH CAKE/MONEY WOULD MAKE YOU FEEL BEST IN THE FREEZER, THE FRIDGE, AND ON THE TABLE?

WHAT WOULD IT LOOK LIKE OR FEEL LIKE IF ALL YOUR MONEY WASN'T ALWAYS INSTANTLY ACCESSIBLE?

The Prosperity Problem

I know more people who have more problems with prosperity than any other theological topic. There have certainly been times where there has been misuse, abuse, and manipulation of this subject. However, I also believe that we have thrown out the baby with the bath water with this.

The root of this theology isn't just simply that God wants you to prosper, but rather people get held up on the moments where the idea of sowing and reaping comes up. That's often when some feathers and feelings can get a tad ruffled. What's interesting to me, is that many who are against any sort of idea that God wants you taken care of, or those who are simply against any idea of prosperity and God being connected, often seem to have less money. There are always a few outliers, but in my experience, the people who are the loudest people booing are the ones living in the cheapest, grape jelly seats.

It's grape jelly for you to neglect the prosperity that God has for you.

I get to be generous, and due to my generosity, my poverty breaks, and prosperity follows. You will get out of poverty at the speed in which you give out in generosity.

I do not condone or believe in asking people to give $100 and it'll turn into $10,000, but I am into the idea of telling people that there is a divine opportunity to enter into an abundant life. It just happens to be tied to your generosity. The best part is that you don't have to. You don't have to give and you don't have to sow. On the other side of that, you also don't have to be blessed.

> You will get out of poverty at the speed in which you give out in generosity.

Jesus gives a teaching about just this. It's a parable about talents (the weight of a measure of gold, silver, or other valuable substances). Some of you reading this have a talent for trying to say that Jesus wants you to be poor. Jesus doesn't make you or want you poor. Your poor choices are what make you poor. Poor choices create poor people. Your poverty is tied to your past, while your prosperity is tied to God's future for you. God wants what you want more than even you want it.

You'll never see prosperity tied to your giving if that's why you're giving. Let this be said. Your reaping isn't tied to the size of your sowing. It's tied to size of your life and how much you give in relation to that. The woman who gave her last token gave more than those who gave thousands, because she gave her all. **Too many of us give what's left and don't give what's right.**

There has been a shift over the years, as many have abused the idea of prosperity. At one point prosperity was constantly talked about and taught on, then it had some people abuse it and manipulate other, to a point now where people are so afraid of doing the wrong thing, they don't do anything in teaching on this. Now people often teach the same thing, but we call it generosity so as to not make people feel uncomfortable. Let me set the record straight. Your generosity can only flow out of your prosperity.

WHAT JESUS SAYS ABOUT PROSPERITY

The first miracle that Jesus did was a provisional miracle. The first miracle recorded in the Bible happened when Jesus was at a wedding (I would love to see Jesus' wedding dance moves). When they ran out of wine, Jesus turned water into wine. You can live without wine, but you can't live without water. **Jesus turned what we needed into something that we wanted. Jesus wanted the party to go on.**

GRAPE JELLY

It's wild to me that Jesus doesn't just meet our needs, but He wants to be a part of our wants too. In all reality, Jesus wants what you want more than you want it.

THE STICKY AND SWEET OF PROSPERITY

Whether you came from money or you came from money problems, you need to get a fresh understanding that where you were doesn't dictate where you're going. Put in the hard, uncomfortable work to be in a better position than those who have come before you. Success can feel strange once you've reached it, but you don't need survivor's guilt to cover your success. You deserve to win, even if that makes the people who aren't winning around you uncomfortable. In reality, the people who are frustrated when you win in the game of finance are those who are only upset at themselves. When they see you, they see what's possible, and they haven't done anything to do what's possible. Too many people are living in an attitude of grape jelly, but doesn't mean you have to. While everyone else is living in grape jelly, my belief is that you're called to prosperity.

Anyone who tells you otherwise is only saying that because, he or she is living in mindset of poverty. Those who live grape jelly hate seeing others who aren't.

God wants to put His hand on your life, and when that happens, nothing that comes against you will prosper. That's literally a verse in the Bible. Some of us are still living in poverty, living that grape jelly life where we're constantly striving to make something happen instead of being obedient to the God. This isn't about being lazy and watching God. It's about doing what you need to do while you let God do what He wants to do. If I can be so honest, the only reason people hate prosperity is because they're still living in poverty. They're still in their grape jelly story.

SO NOW WHAT?

I have two quick questions for you. The first is this: do you believe that God wants you to be healthy? Most everyone would say yes, and that's true, God wants you in good health, so you can fulfill His divine purpose for your life. The second question is this: do you believe that God wants you to be wealthy? This question is where I typically lose about half of a room. Many believe God wants to heal our bodies and make us healthy; yet those same people often don't believe the same for their finances.

You deserve more. You deserve better. The only people who I hear that don't want more, or don't want better, are people who haven't experienced it. In this chapter, we're going to dive into some ideas of prosperity. I have never heard a wealthy person complain about prosperity. I only ever hear poor people complain about prosperity.

Let me make this straight. I do not think that if you give X amount of money, then you will automatically get X amount more of that money. However, I do believe what the Bible says about sowing and reaping in a healthy context. This passage is something that has changed my life.. Jesus uses this parable to teach a lesson, and I want to break it down, so we can understand why some have more than others, and how we can step into an area of faithful finances.

I want to paraphrase what Jesus tells us and then take it apart section by section directly from the Bible so that you can see for yourself what Jesus is saying. The general idea is that the master has three servants. He entrusts different amounts of wealth to them, and it says He determined that by their ability to steward it. There are three men, and they get three different amounts due to their ability. The master leaves, and after a while comes back. Two of the men invested the money, so that it doubled. The man with 5 ended with 10, and the man with 2 ended up with 4. The last person was given one, but instead of investing and sowing it into something that would produce more, he ended up hiding it. The master saw all this when he got back and was excited with the men who doubled his money. But he was furious with the one who hid the single amount. What ends up happening is that the man with one talent is told to give his one to that man who was given 5. So, let's take a deeper look at the message itself that Jesus shares.

> To one he gave five talents, to another two, to another one, to each **according to his ability.**
> Matthew 25:14-29

This is an incredibly powerful verse to me, one the most important when it comes to our stewardship of God's finances. It's easy to see that Jesus is parabolically showing us how God (the master) gives us (the servants) money to steward. I don't know about you, but growing up, it always seemed like everyone else had more money. It seemed like most other people outside of my friend group were other kids of lesser means families. That's something in itself. If you have money, you should hang out with people who both have and don't have. If you are someone without money, do the same. Learn from the mistakes of those who have not, and the lessons from those who have.

The majority of people who have wealth don't get it from a will or inheritance. Most wealth is created.

When I read this passage, it shows me two things. First that God entrusts those who trust Him, and secondly that God knows what He's doing when He's giving people more. We only have as much money as we are able to steward. So, when I feel like I don't have as much as I should, what I probably have is the amount in which I am able to handle.

Then he went away. He who had received the five talents went at once and traded with them, and he made five talents more. So also he who had the two talents made two talents more. But he who had received the one talent went and dug in the ground and hid his master's money. Now after a long time the master of those servants came and settled accounts with them. And he who had received the five talents came forward, bringing five talents more, saying, 'Master, you delivered to me five talents; here, I have made five talents more.' His master said to him, 'Well done, good and faithful servant. You have been faithful over a little; I will set you over much. Enter into the joy of your master.' And he also who had the two talents came forward, saying, 'Master, you delivered to me two talents; here, I have made two talents more.' His master said to him, 'Well done, good and faithful servant. You have been faithful over a little; I will set you over much. Enter into the joy of your master.' He also who had received the one talent came forward, saying, 'Master, I knew you to be a hard man, reaping where you did not sow, and gathering where you scattered no seed, so I was afraid, and I went and hid your talent in the ground. Here, you have what is yours.' But his master answered him, 'You wicked and slothful servant! You knew that I reap where I have not sown and gather where I scattered no seed? Then you ought to have invested my money with the bankers, and at my coming I should have received what was my own with interest. So take the talent from him and give it to him who has the ten talents. For to everyone who has will more be given, and he will have an abundance. But from the one who has not, even what he has will be taken away (Matthew 25:16-21).

Here is a phrase I hear all the time, "The rich get richer, and the poor get poorer." I most often hear this phrase from people who have a negative tone toward the idea. When you hear the statement, does it excite you or does it frustrate you? This will give you a good glimpse at your view of wealth and money in general. If, when you hear that the rich get richer, it frustrates you, it's because you have a poor mentality. If you had a rich mentality, you'd be excited about that statement.

If you see that statement, and it upsets you, it's because you believe that you are poor and you can't get out of it. You're right. If you think you can never get out of being poor, then you likely won't. What we often do is the same as the man with the smallest. We get a little bit of money, and then we hide it. We keep it as safe as we can, so as not to lose it or spend it.

HEALTHY SOWING

The measure in which you have is the measure in which you should give. The parable that Jesus tells isn't that someone is given 5 talents and sowed 10, because that would be foolish, and the math wouldn't add up. On the other side of it, they didn't receive 5 and sow only 3. This doesn't mean that you should give all of your money away, but it does mean that you should measure your giving. **Your manner of living should determine your manner of giving.**

Suppose you have a big house, fantastic. If you drive a sports car, cool. Do you stay at 5-star hotels? Good for you. However, don't stay at 5-star hotels only to give motels. It's okay to have much, but your giving should match your lifestyle. Give hotel stays, not motel stays.

GRAPE JELLY

It's okay to have wealth; **God never got upset at King David over his wealth.** It's okay to have much, just give to that measure.

This is why you should plan out your giving. Our monthly budget after tithing is our giving. Your tithe (10%) goes to your storehouse (local church), while giving goes wherever you believe it should go. Let me mention a pet peeve of mine. I occasionally hear people saying that they tithe 12%. That is literally impossible. Tithe in the original biblical language means a tenth. If you 'tithe 12%' what you really do is return, or tithe, 10% while you then give 2%.

You don't have to give, but you also don't have to reap. They are intrinsically connected. A farmer can't complain he or she has no crop when he or she never planted any seeds. We limit God to our level of faith when we do this. Let's have some faith in what is true: God wants what you want, more than you want it.
One single passage of scripture sums this all this up. Proverbs 11:24:
> *"One gives freely, yet, grows all the richer; another withholds who he should give, and only suffers want." The fastest way to grow all the richer is to give freely.*

LEARNING TO REAP

When my wife and I were in the beginning of our pregnancy with our son, the cravings were out of this world.

Ice cream was the main culprit. Technically, I was the one with cravings. My wife Rebecca didn't have a single craving during her pregnancy (talk about an unmet expectation). For the whole pregnancy, I wanted her to feel like she had permission to crave, so I paved the way. One of these times, we were randomly driving, and I saw a Dairy Queen up ahead. I, being a good husband, mentioned that we should stop. We pulled into the drive through, ordered our blizzards, and headed up to pay for them. We got to the window, and the employee told us that the person in front of us had paid for our ice cream. In fact, this had been going on for many cars. My wife looked at me, then I looked back at the Dairy Queen lady, and I did what anyone would do. I took the free ice cream and drove away.

A couple weeks later, we went out to brunch by our house, and the same thing happened. We ate all of the food. The eggs, the bacon, the cinnamon roll, all of it. The waitress came by and said that our meal had been taken care of for us. We looked around to see if it was someone we knew and couldn't find anyone that we knew. We asked the waitress who it was, and she said that the person had already left. He had just wanted to pay for someone's meal. The best part though was that when the waitress then asked if we wanted to pay for someone else's meal, I said no thanks, and we left.

You may read that and be disgusted and confused. The truth is that there weren't multiple cars that were giving. It was multiple cars passing along the payment. There weren't a lot of tables being blessed with free food. They were just passing along the expense. It only became giving once someone actually received the blessing. I am okay with receiving blessings, and you should be too.

I find it really fascinating how many people we try to give to, who won't receive it, or don't receive it well. If you'd say it's hard for you to receive gifts, then I want to help you out and maybe even help you discover where that derives from. Here is a major issue. If you can't receive $5 from someone, but you're praying for someone to pay off your debt or give you a house, you've got it all backwards, and honestly, it's just wrong.

At the end of the story, the master in the story says that to those who are able to deal with a little will be blessed with more. "Whoever can be trusted with very little can also be trusted with much, and whoever is dishonest with very little will also be dishonest with much." You know who said that? Jesus (Luke 16:10). Jesus wants to entrust you with more, but how can he give you more when you won't receive less.

> How can he give you more when you won't receive less?

So many of us, myself included, start our relationship with money from our family of origin. If you saw your family give, then you're probably a giver. If you never saw that, then it might be a whole new thing for you to learn to enjoy. You may have even been brought up in a family that wouldn't receive help or giving from others because it would be a cultural anomaly to do so.

My hope is that if you saw giving that you give more than you've seen given. If you never saw giving, then you get to start a new lifestyle and family blessing of stepping into a new season of giving. Let me say again that tithing isn't giving. You're not a giver when you tithe. You're just someone who doesn't steal. That's the minimum expectation. Giving is anything you do outside of the tithe.

WHY YOU DON'T RECEIVE WELL

1. YOU DON'T FEEL LIKE YOU DESERVE IT.

I would say in my personal experience that at least nine out of ten times, when I try to give people anything, I have to offer it at least twice before they receive it. If you think it's polite to reject a blessing, then you're living a grape jelly life where you don't think you deserve better. **Rejecting a blessing isn't a common courtesy. It is a blatant insecurity.**

"You don't have to do that."

2. YOU HAVE PRIDE THAT SAYS YOU DON'T NEED IT.

This is one makes me laugh a little when it happens. One thing that is beyond fun is paying for someone's groceries for the person behind you. What's wild to me though is the amount of times that I don't have success with being able to do so. Often, if not the majority of the time, I will have people tell me that they don't need any help financially, and they are fine.

Since when did receiving have to be based on need? You don't need to be blessed. That's why it's called a blessing not a need. Pride is a killer of wealth. Pride rejects blessings and budgets, because you don't feel like you need them. Why wait until you need something in order to receive it?

3. YOU HAVEN'T FULLY UNDERSTOOD SALVATION

I believe that Jesus is very real. He is the son of the living God, who came on this Earth, lived a perfect life, and then died in my place for me. I accepted that when I was young. I then accepted it when I was a teenager. Salvation actually became a daily ritual when I was in high school. I was "getting saved" and asking forgiveness as if that were my daily devotional.

The best thing about the gift of salvation is just that. It's a gift. You can't earn it, you don't deserve it, but it's for you. Jesus wants to give you life, and life abundantly (John 10:10). Jesus wants what you want, more than you even want it. He wants you to have salvation in Him. What would it look like if we started receiving blessings in the same way that we receive salvation?

Many receive salvation easier than gifts. I see this all the time. I speak at conferences and give opportunities to pray for salvation, and I've seen countless thousands of people say yes to that. I've also, in those same events, tried to give away books I have written. Some of those very same people refuse to receive them and demand they pay for them. Now I'm not going to fight anyone trying to give me money, so I take that payment.

I wonder if Jesus would reject blessings as often as we do? I don't think so. If anything, Jesus sees those who give and thinks highly of them, from the woman who gave the most to the woman who poured out all of her expensive perfume. You know what I love? Jesus didn't tell the lady not to pour it because it was expensive.

Now I already feel it, "But that's Jesus, He deserves everything." True, and you become benefactors of God's benefits when receive Jesus. Do you deserve all that Jesus does? No. Did Jesus deserve all that we gave him on the cross? No. Yet this is the life we have the opportunity to live.

HOW TO RECEIVE WELL

1. GET OVER YOURSELF

I don't know of any other way to say it. First and foremost, if you need help receiving then you need to understand that you may be more blessed than you realized. If you struggle with getting gifts or having dinner paid for, and you simply feel like you don't deserve it, then you need to get over your past, so that God can bless your future. The road to move forward isn't easy, but it is blessed.

2. GIVE WELL

The best way to see the benefits of receiving is to be on the other end of it. When you start giving and see the life change on the other side of your giving, it'll make you want to be on the other side of other's giving.

3. SAY THANK YOU

So often when we give, we see people make excuses for why they need our generosity. Those people are mixing up charity with generosity. They can look similar but the heart is different. Charity is based on need. Giving and generosity are based on abundance and prosperity toward and from others. The best way to receive well is to simply just receive and say thank you. You don't have to explain or push away. You can simply receive.

GIVING WHEN PEOPLE ARE BAD AT RECEIVING

When I was a kid there was something that we loved to do when the two of us would go out to eat. We would pay for someone else's meal without them knowing about it. One time we did this, and it was the biggest fail of all time. We were at a restaurant in Midland, Michigan where we were living at the time. We were having our meal and enjoying it, and we noticed that in the corner of the establishment there was a family that consisted of a dad, mom, and one daughter. That daughter looked like she was having the worst day of her life. We took notice and with great excitement, we asked the waiter if we could pay for that table's bill. Of course, this was easy for me, because technically my dad was paying for it to bless someone else.

We watched as anonymous givers with great anticipation for the family to get excited. We also wanted to do something extra for the daughter because she looked so unhappy, so we told the waitress to also tell the girl she could order any dessert she wanted, and it would also be covered. So cool, right? What could go wrong?

We saw the waitress walk over to the table and have the conversation about what was going on. There seemed to be little reaction, but we were cool with that. Our reaction was not the goal of giving. **You can't let how someone receives determine how you give.** What happened next, we still can't get over, and it's been decades. The waitress brought the dessert to the girl, and immediately the parents took her plate of dessert and ate the entire thing. She wasn't allowed to have any.

I wonder as I type this, because of how random and awful those parents were, but also I wonder if there is a lady out there now who has this traumatic story of when her bad day got worse, because we sent over dessert that she never got to eat.

My dad paid for the bill and the dessert with his money, but I got to experience the joy of giving and seeing what it does when we give. That's just how it is with our heavenly father. When we tithe, we operate and step into a heavenly economy where we can and should give on a regular basis just because we can. When we give and obey God, we don't just live a blessed life, but we get to help others have blessed moments.

On the other side of this, would you ever go to a place, eat the food, and expect that you wouldn't have to pay for it just because you weren't feeling it? Of course not. You pay regardless. Yet so many believers attend church and don't pay a tithe every month. The most recent statistic I heard was that over 90% of people who attend a church (storehouse) do not obey the Lord in their tithe. This means that the majority of believers are in disbelief and are under a curse (Malachi 3:8-10).

Don't be like those people. Be a faithful person and step out in faith. Then, see if God won't open up the gates of heaven for you, your children, and your generations to come.

IT'S NOT ON YOU TO MAKE IT HAPPEN

At the end of the day prosperity has some parts to do with us sowing, giving, and being generous humans. However, the reaping, the prosperity of it all is on God. So often we try to work our ways into be blessed instead of letting God do the labor. My prayer for you is that you might reap where you haven't sown. Sowing just makes the harvest greater.

If you're the one who's calling you to be blessed, then it's on you to make it happen. If God is the one calling you to be blessed, it's on Him to make it happen. You can do whatever you want, but as for me and my house, we will serve the Lord who has always been faithful, fruitful, and has never let us down.

I DON'T AGREE WITH YOU

You don't have to agree with me. I give you permission to disagree with me or to think I'm insane, but at the end of the day, I know that I'm living in abundance of time, resource, and freedom, and it's all tied to what I give away.

It's wild to me that the thing that holds so many back from prosperity is their lack of giving. It's like a rich young ruler syndrome. You're so afraid you'll lose all you've made for yourself that you keep it to yourself, so it never goes where it was made to go.

Can I be honest? The only reason someone would disagree that Jesus has more for them is because they either don't know the Word, or they think too small of themselves. There's an entire passage of scripture that talks about how God feeds and clothes birds and plants, so how much more will He take care of you? The Holy Spirit is not a bird, and neither are you. He loves you more than the birds that are taken care of.

GRAPE JELLY

Reflection

WHAT HAS PROSPERITY LOOKED LIKE FOR YOU IN THE PAST?

DOES IT HAVE POSITIVE OR NEGATIVE CONNOTATIONS?

WHAT'S THE BIGGEST THING HOLDING YOU BACK FROM A PROSPEROUS LIFE?

How to Get a Free House

Jesus wants you to be blessed. Does He want you to be rich beyond measure? Probably not. I think we often do things that put a hold on our blessings. I believe a blessed financial life is on hold for many because of one way of our thinking: comparison.

I realized that I was holding myself back from being blessed when I was frustrated that someone was more blessed than I was. We've all been there, right? Just me? Cool. I ended up making these spiritual equations in my head to find the reason or the excuse for God to bless someone more than He was currently blessing me. Many people of influence in our lives have been given cars, vacations, and even houses – 100% given to them by another person.

GRAPE JELLY

We had some friends over at our house and they ended up telling us that someone, whom they had no real
knowledge of beforehand, gave them a house. This
wasn't a house that was falling apart. If anything, it's
one of the the coolest places I've seen in my life. Can I
be honest? They told us this, and a part of me died inside. I was frustrated, not with them, but with God. The
catch was this though. They were in the middle of taking a massive step of obedient faith when this happened.
They were being radically blessed by their radical speed
of obedience.

My wife was freaking out with excitement for our friends.
I was faking it until I could make it. I really was thrilled
for my friends, but I felt a deeper frustration over the
good news. I had to seek God about it and figure out
why on earth I was so frustrated, envious, and confused.
If I'm honest, I was hurt, because I felt like God didn't
care for me as much as he was caring for my friends.
That's grape jelly.

WE MAKE OUR PURCHASES WHEN COMPARING

I travel an inordinate amount of times in a year which
means, I'm in an airport multiple times a week. As my
travel schedule continues to be busy, more and more, I
see people with terrible jobs dress to the nines. Get ready
for my hot take.

These are young people who have terrible jobs working
at the airport either cleaning bathrooms or taking out the

trash. **Those jobs are terrible. Someone has to do them, but it doesn't have to be you.** I have seen too many times where someone who is making the absolute minimum is wearing shoes that cost the maximum. I've seen people who make an hourly wage, yet they wear clothes that might cost them not hours, but days or weeks of earning to afford. **You don't deserve things that you can't afford.** Many people have nice shoes even though they make no money. Become a better self by getting over yourself.

I ended up figuring out that I would never have the faith for our home to be paid for or paid off without first seeing it happen. In full transparency, the more I see people receive cars, houses, vacations and opportunities, it doesn't make me want what they received, but rather it makes me want to give like the one who gave it to them. Seeing blessings and generosity can make you more generous.

OUR FIRST HOME

We have a crazy story for ourselves when it comes to how we bought our first home. This is the irony of the story really. I was jealous of my friends who were given a home, when we were told the news in a home that in many ways was given to us, not in full, but we know God made the way for this house.

My wife and I closed on our first home in the first year of our marriage, and that's not something that I think is normal or should it be. The story of this home started before we were married. Rebecca and I had just recently gotten engaged, and we were hanging out at my parents' house one evening. A little while after it had gotten dark, Rebecca took off and headed to her apartment. Everything was quite normal. Then out of nowhere, I felt this nudge to call Rebecca and see how her drive was doing. It was either the Lord guiding me or me trying to flirt on the phone. Either way she answered.

She picked up the phone sobbing saying she was just in a huge car accident on the highway. I started driving as fast as I could. Just a couple minutes later, and I saw the flashing lights and saw Rebecca's car smashed up against the trees past the side of the highway. Her car was totaled along with two other vehicles. I ran to Rebecca and held her tighter than I think I have ever held any human being. She began to tell me that she was hit by a man who I could see out the corner of my eyes, handcuffed. He was driving on the wrong side of the highway completely inebriated. He ended up slamming into a truck and then into Rebecca's car. That truck took most of the blow and completely saved Rebecca's life, but even so, her car was destroyed by the second hit the car did to hers.

Rebecca ended up having some injuries, and over time become alright. Within the process from issues to being alright were doctor's visits, chiropractor visits, and the like, all that cost money and large amounts of it. During all of this, insurance claims started happening, and we were advised by some to hire a lawyer for all it. After everything was said and done, not only were the doctors' visits covered, but Rebecca walked away with multiple tens of thousands of dollars from the settlement by the drunk driver's insurance.

So, we went out and bought a couple of jet skis.

Not really, but how crazy would that be if you read that whole story and then realized we bought jet skis. We did what anyone should do when they receive a large amount of money and that is that first we tithed, and then we went to our financial advisor and asked, what should we do? This started the process of us getting our first home. It gets so much better.

There is a passage in the Bible where it's paraphrased to say what the enemy made for evil, the Lord will make for good. We were just in the beginning stage of under-standing that passage.

We started looking for a house, and we ended up having what I would consider a normal house hunting experience. We had a budget, and it wasn't based on what the loan officer offered us, but it was based on what we could afford at the current time. We weren't hoping for more money. We were planning out our mortgage based on what it would be like if we never made any more money ever, while knowing that we would make more.

We checked out the house, which may have been the smallest house I had ever been to in my life. Then we went to another house, and the neighborhood was so rough that we never went inside. This was a concerning moment for me. I started thinking to myself like, man I really thought we had enough money for this thing, but I guess houses are just more expensive than I thought. We continued over the coming weeks to check out houses, and most were not places I saw us for at least 5 years, which is a good rule of thumb for buying a house. We ended up going to a house, that represented our all-time low.. There was a dog at the showing, caged up in the living room, just staring at us, and the breed of it I'm pretty sure was a bear. This house was terrible. There was a lot of work that would have to be done, I don't know how to do anything like that.

Rebecca and I were discouraged. We had this belief that we would have manyGod moments while looking for a house, since the downpayment we planned for was already given to us through the insurance. Now, we wanted to go back to our one bedroom, one bathroom apartment. We actually had a theme song that we would sing when we drove up to our apartment: "Where the gates are always open." Because this gated apartment complex constantly had the gates broken, so that anyone could just drive in.

We wanted to go back to this not so great first apartment, but our realtor looked at us and said, "We can't give up. There is one more showing I have for us today, and I think you'll really like it." We did like it. We liked it so much that by the end of the day, we had put in an offer for the house, above the asking price, because we loved it so much.

We knew we had this house. We had faith and also the simple understanding that if you offer $10,000 over the asking price that you would for sure get the house. We didn't get the house. We actually never even heard from them. We were so discouraged, so let down, that we started hating looking at houses. We had already fallen in love.

I remember the first time I felt like this. I was 15 years old, and I had just gotten into my first boyfriend/girl-friend relationship (I was the boyfriend just to be clear). I was so convinced that she was going to be my wife because I had never felt this way before. Have you ever been there? I feel like this happens to me often that I get emotionally connected before I know enough to be com-mitted. I prayed a prayer saying, "God, let this girl be my wife." That's how much faith I had in this. We ended up breaking up over a year later. It devastated me be-cause in my mind, this was my wife. (I am now married to the greatest woman ever, just for the record).

The same was true for this house. I kept thinking while we were checking out other houses that I already found the one. This house had all that we needed: two bed-rooms, two bathrooms, a closet that could hold our washer and dryer, and a decent living room. We were all in on this house.

Then we pulled up to a house our realtor showed us online. It really seemed too good to be true, but we checked it out. As we were driving close to the house, we could see a lot of construction, and realized that there was a massive multi-million dollar development being built within walking distance to this house we were checking out. So now we were just angry.. We loved a house, haven't heard anything back from this house in weeks, and now we were being shown a house that we for sure couldn't get.

We stepped into the house, and it made our first love look like my first girlfriend. I am so glad that didn't work out! We walked around the house, and we didn't leave the house until we made an offer. This house blew away everything about the past house. It had three bedrooms, three bathrooms, not a laundry closet but a whole room, and then a whole extra room in the front of the house, all for the same cost as the one we fell in love with before.

The story gets wild from here.

We heard back not a day later that the owners accepted our offer on the houses. That's right, the houses. Plural. What had happened regarding that the first house we fell in love with and kept praying for is that they accepted our offer right away but let the wrong person know, so they were waiting for weeks for our response to their approval. We actually had it the whole time. At that same time, we found a better home, a home we could start a family in and be in for a much longer time with more room, better area, and walking distance to a multi-million dollar development.

We ended up getting the house. We paid the same amount of money as we offered for the first house got so much more out of it. What I find so funny was that I got so frustrated that God wasn't answering our prayers, until I realized that God sometimes isn't answering our prayers because He has a better plan in mind for us.

What the enemy made for evil, the lord made for good. The truth is, in God's hands, intended evil becomes eventual good.

THE IRONY

The irony is that when our friends told us that they were given a house, I was jealous of them, while I was standing in the house that was provided for us. The problem and the irony with jealousy is that we are always jealous of the things we compare with. It's similar to when kids open a gift, and it's amazing, until their sibling opens up what seems to be a bigger gift. All of the sudden, the gift you are given seems less than. The truth is that when we compare, our gifts turn to garbage, and we never operate in gratitude.

HOW TO STOP COMPARING

The principal way to stop comparing is to start celebrating. I have learned that's hard to be jealous of the people for whom you are cheering when they win. If I'm really truthful, there are some people, and even ministries, that I financially support because originally, I was jealous of them. I figured that the best way to avoid jealousy was to be on the same team. Now when they win, so do I.

You can't compare yourself with what you celebrate.

Just as it's important to give and receive well in your own life, it's just as, if not more, important, when you see others give and receive, that you see it well. The fastest way to lose what you have is to be jealous of things that you don't. This is why it's so bizarre to see people, who I know have very little wealth, drive fancy cars or wear ultra brand name clothing, while they end up living in terrible housing. I see this all the time. You can drive by areas of low income, but their cars won't reflect it.

The best way to stop comparing is to start celebrating, while the second best way is to stop caring. Nobody cares what clothes you wear, car you drive, or about your vacation photos. If they do care, it's because they're shallow. It's hard to have a deep relationship with people who have shallow standards of success. Let's be honest. Someone else's addition isn't your subtraction.

At the end of the day, perspective heals a comparative spirit. **You are always in someone else's envy.** If you have any worldview whatsoever, you'll understand that if you were able to buy this book, you're very likely to be in the top 1% of wealth in the entire world. When your global perspective gets bigger, your problems get smaller. The next moment you start wishing you had more, think about how many people wish they had what you have. This isn't to guilt yourself. It's to better value yourself. When you do this, your pride for what you own increases, while you become humble at the same time. It's one of the only times healthy pride and humility coexist.

Someone else's addition isn't your subtraction.

HOW TO GET A FREE HOUSE

My friends got a free house. I used to be jealous, but then I realized I have a better life than I deserve, so I'm likely in my past self's jealousy and envy. The moment I went from comparison to cheering on those whom I was jealous of, I joined their team. Their win is now my win. Technically, I didn't get a free house, but in many ways, I feel the same joy of having a free house, because the people who I'm cheering for have a free house.

If my past self could see me now, he'd be envious. I pray that you might have a perspective that kills your habit of comparison. I hope you get a free house or can cheer someone on who gets one. For me, my goal isn't to get a free house but is to one day give a free house to someone. I'd rather put my focus on giving than getting. Just a thought.

GRAPE JELLY

Reflection

**WHO IS THE PERSON YOU MOST OFTEN COMPARE
YOURSELF TO AND WHY?**

**WHAT WOULD HAPPEN IF YOU BLESSED THAT
PERSON FINANCIALLY?**

Money and Others

Money doesn't complicate things, people complicate things. One of my many money pet peeves is when I hear people say, "Money just complicates things, I'd rather not talk about it." I grew up in a home, in which my dad would always be honest about finances. I knew how much he made and knew what the Friday night pizza budget was. All I had to do was ask.

Whether it's marriage, family of origin, or kids, money can be an empowering part of . I've seen times of great abundance, incredible hardship, and have seen God's faithfulness through all of it. This chapter is a quick breakdown of some easy wins for you in regard to money with others in our circles.

GRAPE JELLY

PART ONE: MARRIAGE

In my marriage we've seen the highs and lows of money. However, as long as you have enough money for a pizza night once in a while, you'll be okay. I mean let's be honest, pizza is cheap and makes everyone happy. Pizza fixes all problems. Okay so maybe not all problems, but it helps.

Marriage and money should be one of the most exciting times of your financial journey, because you get to share the journey with the one you love the most. The problems come into play when you love your money more than your marriage. Many can fall into this trap easier than they fell in love their spouse. So, here are three signs to notify you that you may love money more than your marriage.

3 SIGNS YOU LOVE MONEY MORE THAN YOUR MARRIAGE

1. You have separate bank accounts.
2. Only one of you makes the financial decisions.
3. You have a prenup.

Having separate bank accounts is one of the fastest ways to say, *I don't trust you.* When only one of you makes the financial decisions, that is the quickest way to say *I know better than you.* Lastly, and probably most painfully, is that if you have a prenuptial agreement in your marriage, you are saying, *I have an exit strategy.* Or that I care more about my money than you. It's narcissistic.

Doing any or all of these three things is like getting on a plane wearing a parachute. Can you do it? Yes. Does it make everyone else concerned? For sure. When you're married, you need to get on that plane without a parachute, without a backup plan. Every time someone has a plan b, they always end up using it.

When you have separate bank accounts, only one of you makes all the calls. If you have a prenup, this all points to one thing: you aren't committed to the marriage. I know this, because the Bible says that where your treasure is, so is your heart also. If you don't trust your spouse with "your money," then you probably aren't a great spouse. There's a way out of this though.

HOW TO SOLVE MONEY PROBLEMS IN MARRIAGE

At the start of this book, I went through the three money stories we can be in: Theirs, Yours, and Gods. However, there is a fourth money story. Ours.

> Every time someone has a plan b, they always end up using it.

For most of us, we move from their money story to our money, to God's money story. **If you're married, what should happen is that *your* money story turns into *our* money story.** A quick move in this direction is to first acknowledge and apologize for any aspect of dic-

GRAPE JELLY

tatorship when you should have a democracy of mutual ownership with money in marriage. There is typically one person who is more financially fit and is better with the numbers. However, leading doesn't mean dictatorship. If anything, it gives you an opportunity to lead toward the alignment of your mutual goals.

My last advice for marriage is this. It'll change the whole game for you with your marriage in regard to money. Ask your spouse, **"Do you feel like a team when it comes to our money?"** In this simple question, you're addressing the idea that the money is *our money*. You're giving your spouse room to speak about money, and you're putting yourself in a vulnerable situation, in which you can address problems and change accordingly. Your future marriage will thank you.

PART TWO: KIDS

As I write this, my son is less than a year old. My advice: listen to people who have actual experience in the subject you need help in. Hit me up in 10 years if you have teens or young adults in your family.

We do have plans to teach our kids about what it's like to be blessed and the power of generosity, but for now we mainly look to others for wisdom in this area.

PART THREE: FAMILY

Money should be talked about. Whether it's with your

parents, in laws, or second cousin who is twice removed (whatever that even means), I would love for people to be more open about conversations with money. I rarely understand the idea of money being private. The biggest reveal to me happens when someone is struggling with their money, and they don't want to talk about it. The irony is, the only way you get better with your money is by talking about it.

If your family makes more than you, learn from them. If your family makes less than you, learn from them. You'll never learn from people you don't talk to though.

PART FOUR: FRIENDS

Money can be your friend without it ruining your friendships. However, there are always those out there who will try to leverage your relationship for financial gain. These people are called fools.

I have an acquaintance from college (not a friend, you'll see why shortly) who calls me once a year to "reconnect." He'll hit me up, ask me how things are going, and every year he asks me about my situation, not really listening to me. Then there is always a transitional statement that goes something like this: "So anyway, I want to talk to you about this incredible opportunity." Here's my thing, if you have a great opportunity, good for you. You want to share about it, that's fine. However, if you call me every year with a different opportunity of how to get rich quick, I have to look at your track record and maybe, just maybe, you have zero idea what you're doing with your life. Real friends don't ask you to be in multi-level marketing or pyramid schemes. If I'm honest, it's just rude. If you're my friend and need money, just ask.

The other way people are often bad friends with money is when you ask your friend for a discount. I have friends who own businesses, and I want to support my friends. I want to fully support them. I don't want to discount support them. Pay full price for your friends' work. Pay other's the same way you'd like to be paid.

Being a good friend with money is a lot more fun, so be a good friend. One of the greatest ways to be a good friend is to celebrate those who are winning more than you. I have friends who make substantially more than I do. I have friends who make what I paid for my house multiple times over in a single year. The friends in my life that have nicer things, bigger houses, and larger bank accounts, I celebrate them. I want my friends to win. Celebrate others the way you'd want to be celebrated.

PEOPLE AND MONEY

God wants to show you what is possible through others. When you family, friends, and even strangers that have more wealth than you, God might be trying to show you what's possible if you live your life in accordance to His standards. **Your standards of living shouldn't be compared to your earthly neighbor, but rather celebrated in glory to your heavenly Father.**

Reflection

HOW DO YOU FEEL WHEN YOU TALK TO OTHERS ABOUT MONEY?

WHY DO YOU THINK YOU FEEL THAT WAY?

GRAPE JELLY

Budget for the Blessing

My wife and I still have the notebook where we drafted the first budget we ever made together when we were engaged. To look at it now it scares me to death! I wonder how we ever ate more than peanut butter and jelly sandwiches living on so little. I love having that as a remembrance of where God has taken us from financially to where we are at now. I also believe that in a decade from now we will laugh at the current budget we have. We are making sure of that by having a budget. **A budget is a plan for your future you can look back on and see how blessed you currently are if you use it correctly.**

Your goals determine your future, and your budget determines how you get to your goals. **You need to tell**

your money where to go before it tells you where it went. The main reason people struggle with debt is because they don't have goals, and then they don't have budgets for those goals. Debt is when your purchases tell your money where to go..

When it comes to budgeting, your goals are the pillars that hold it together. Your free goal, your giving goal, and your end goal will help you understand why you are budgeting the way you are budgeting. Let's say we have a free goal of getting out of all debt (house, student loans, cars). Your budget would then focus on that. You control the budget, so that the money doesn't control you.

If you want to be able to have more budge in your budget, figure out how to hustle in addition to your primary source of income. There were many times that I was flying to go speak somewhere, and I am paid to do that. However, since I am driving to the airport anyway, I would leave a little bit before I normally would and I will pick up other people who are heading to the airport using a ride share company. I would make money on my trip to go and make money. Same with going to a meeting in the city or going to a friend's house in another city. We create the budge in our budget by doing things other people aren't doing.

The first thing you need to do is tithe, and if you aren't doing that, your budget will never work for you, you'll be working for it. Tithe to God what already belongs to

Him. Do that first. I encourage people not to have this set up automatically. I think there is a good need in the human nature of giving, in whatever venue in which you do it. However, when you automate it, you never feel it. I don't know about you, but I want to feel the tithe.

The second category would be how we choose to give. Some of our giving is spontaneous, and some of it is structured. One thing that we have been doing for our entire marriage is that we sponsor a girl in a country of far less means that the one we live in. We currently pay $38 a month, and that gives her school, food, and medical attention. We spend $38 on a meal let alone an entire month of them.

After you know how much you'll tithe and how much you'll give, then there are only a few other main categories. The money you live off for your bills, food, all of that, then your savings, and lastly your investments in whatever categories you choose to do so. Every human needs a budget, so that they tell their money where to go. If you have little money, you need a budget, so you don't have less, and if you have a lot of money, you need it so that you aren't foolish with your funds.

I AM TOO RICH FOR A BUDGET

If you make enough money to have something we call extra, and you have so much of it that you don't feel like you need to budget, you are a fool. Only a fool lets their money make the rules. I have met so many people that make multiple times what I make and yet have half of what I have because they don't have budgets. When you don't have a budget, it's like having a dog that never uses a leash. Can it work? Certainly. A dog can only ever be without a leash long after they've learned how to be with a leash.

You may hate budgets, but if we're honest, you don't hate budgets. You hate restriction. If you do budgets the right way, you won't be restricting yourself, you'll be freeing your future.

HOW RICH IS TOO RICH

Have you ever eaten a piece of cake or dessert and thought, "This is too rich?" Our finances can easily turn into the same problem. When we hoard and gather our funds so that we feel more and more secure for the simple idea of security, that's often when we are most insecure about our situations.

I would venture to say that currently a large majority of my friends make more than I do, and I celebrate them for it. The question can often be though, how much is too much? When I hear people talk about their greatest financial mistakes, it's almost always that they spent too much on too many things. We are all tempted to do it.

If you're in a place where you have abundance and prosperity, awesome. I want that for you. The biggest thing to make sure of is that your giving matches your lifestyle. God isn't providing just for you but also through you. You want Mercedes? Get it. However, you better give like a Mercedes too. Don't live like a Mercedes and give like a Toyota. The measure in which you live should look equal to the measure you give.

HOW TO MAKE A BUDGET IN LESS THAN 5 MINUTES

1. Figure out your average monthly income.
We budget per month and not by year because different seasons require different funding.

2. List your expenses (including tithe and giving). If you don't plan to tithe and give, it won't happen.

3. Make sure you have extra after your expenses.

For many people this may be the most difficult aspect of budgeting. You may feel like you have too much time left over after your paycheck is spent. I understand how frustrating that can be. Of course, the solution is to either make more in side income and side jobs or spend less in places that aren't needs. You may also realize some of what you call needs are just deeper wants. You deserve what you want, but not if it costs you the future that you want more.

That's pretty much it. If you know how much you make in a month, and you have a basic understanding of your monthly expenses, then you're on the right track. I personally categorize my spending, so I see how much money is going where on a more macro level which can be helpful.

If you have your average income, divide that over all your expenses while being sure you have money left-over. Then you can start changing your future. The real trick here is being realistic with your budget and expenses. I change my budget at the end of every month to prepare for the next month, and I go over my budget every single day for a minute or two at most to make sure I'm on track to hit my budget. If you stay within your budget, you will stay on track for your goals.

HOW DO I BUDGET MONEY THAT I DON'T HAVE?

You might not have money now, but if you work hard, and you work on yourself, once you're good enough, the money will find you. Jesus literally says that we are given to according to our ability. So, you need to approve your ability and not just your availability to receive.

The best way to prepare for a blessing isn't just opening your hands. It involves also opening up your potential and doing something. Again, the best way out of not having, is by giving some of it away. Giving cures poverty.

On a more practical level let's say you don't have a stable income. Maybe it varies, fluctuates, or simply isn't where you want it to be. You don't budget based on where you want to be but based on where you are. It's like the people who buy pants they hope they'll fit into one day. You can have dreams, but you budget in reality. So if your income changes or fluctuates, budget based on percentages of categories instead of concrete numbers.

THE VACATION BUDGET

Vacations are great; however, we don't do vacations to escape our lives, we do them to amplify them. If you go on a vacation to leave your problems, you'll come back with bigger problems. This happens because you breathe out, relax, and the weight is off of you for a couple days or maybe even a week. When you get home, the weight is thrown on you that you neglected that whole vacation. This is why when we go on vacation it has to be a goal. The goal is to talk through our next season and also to relax and have a more unique type of fun. The one thing that doesn't usually change for us though is our budget. If your budget has to change in order to go on a vacation, your vacation is too expensive.

I never saw a full tank of gas while I was kid until we went on vacation. It was actually a very memorable moment for me as a kid. Seeing my family so excited about something really excited me. They filled up the car with gas for us to go on vacation. I have this belief that part of the vacation for my family was the ability to say things that they wanted to be able to say all the time. Fill up the tank. Order whatever you want. Statements like that.

However too many of us live like this all the time, and

not just on our vacations and trips. We save up for escape instead of saving up for things that would help us
level up.

HOW TO BUDGET WELL

Having a budget is one thing. Making sure that it's a
good budget is another story. I remember early in our
marriage, our budget looked amazing. On paper, we
were paying off our student loans in months not years.
The issue was that our budgets were just written and
not executed. A budget that isn't based in reality isn't a
budget, it's a dream. A budget, a true one, will keep you
structured knowing where the money is going. Budgets
don't keep you safe. They keep you structured. Safety
doesn't come in budgets. Safety comes when you tithe
and give.

When our budget doesn't add up, when it looks like
ends won't meet, we end up increasing our giving. The
more we've given, the safer we've seemed to be. That's
just us though. You don't have to give, you don't have to
be safe, and you don't have to be blessed.

TEST YOUR BUDGET

The best test of your budget and spending is to tell
someone about it. You know you've made a purchase
that isn't of God when you don't tell anyone about it except those who would justify it. If you have to justify
your spending, you're losing.

Reflection

IF YOUR BUDGET WERE A PERSON, WOULD THAT RELATIONSHIP BE A HEALTHY ONE?

GRAPE JELLY

Please Excuse My Dear Aunt Sallie

I have one major regret in my life. Finishing college. I have a piece of paper that I traded for freedom. Why is it that when I used to say, "I am in debt," it made me feel like I was saying, "My name is Ty, and I'm an alcoholic." In college, I met a relative that I had never heard of. In fact, she's a relative in many of my friends lives as well. She's an aunt to us, and she's ruined so many of our lives. Let's just call her Sallie.

What you have to get an understanding of with debt is that any **debt that doesn't make you more money than it costs is a disease.** It spreads lies and is contagiously spreading into homes, marriages, and everyday lives. When my wife and I first got married, we made very little in terms of compensation, and our debt was taking a large share of our budget.

If you're someone who is attracted to a payment and not the cost, debt is out to get you and probably already has you. If you have to make payments on it, double check yourself to see if you can really afford it. A decent rule of thumb on being able to afford something with payments: if you had to make that payment twice a month, could you?

The goal of being consumer debt free has been, so I can help break off other people's chains. In the 22nd Proverb, it says that the borrower is slave to the lender. The more I read that, the more truth I feel from it. We all have dreams, but your consumer or student debt will derail your dreams from happening when you want them to happen. You may have debt and think it's no issue to you at all. The idea of being a slave to debt may even seem ridiculous. However, if you were to have all your debt taken away what would your life look like? If you can think of how different your life would be and it would change your life even a little bit, then you're currently enslaved to your past purchases, which determine your future preferences.

"But I can afford the payment." That's usually the response when there is any nudge to help people understand their debts. The truth is though that the payment isn't the full cost of your debt. It's costing you time, future, and joy. We too often get so entitled and enthralled by the idea of only having to make payments, but the problem is once you start living a life of payments, you're living in your past purchases.

Debt will keep you in a job that you hate. You'll always be looking forward to retirement instead of living your life for what it should be. Don't get me wrong. We have plans and investments that are looking forward to the time of when we are older in that "retirement age," but we have no plans to ever retire. As a believer in Jesus, we are never called to just quit and let life go by without us pouring into others and continuing our mission on this earth. I laugh when people retire and say they are never going to work again, as if heaven is going to be some sort of place where work and dreams and passions no longer exist. Work will look different when we are older in age, but the goal is for it to be more effective the older we get, so that we enjoy it more and more every day. If your goal is to retire, you may in the wrong job or wrong mindset of why you're on this earth. The people I look up to and that culture looks up to are not those who are waiting for work to be over but those who can't wait for their next work to begin.

If you have debt, no matter your age, one of your top goals should be getting out of it. There is a difference though between you getting out of debt and debt getting out of you.

DEBT IN YOU VS. YOU IN DEBT

Debt starts as a mindset of impatience, lack of wisdom,

or cultural normality. We often believe that debt is the only option for doing so many of things we do.

When you get a raise, do you buy more things, or do you stay put in the life you have and are able to save for the future and the future of others? So many of us end up getting into more debt. The irony of debt is that so many believers in Jesus will obey the tithe, but then they get into debt, which is the opposite of the life Jesus wants us to live. Jesus doesn't want us to be enslaved to a lender or object or payment plan for some random thing.

The mindset of debt needs to be dealt with before you get out of debt. Before you get out of debt, debt needs to get out of you.

We have a mortgage and student loans, but we acknowledge that student loans were a terrible decision that I made because I was 18 when I started getting them with no guidance on what was happening in that. When I started having to pay back my loans, they were all for various return dates, interest rates, and some of them were going to last forever. Of course, all of this is why we ended up consolidating it all for a better way to manage the interest rates and then in turn saving us thousands of dollars over the life of the loan. Life of the loan. What a funny phrase for something that is killing so many people's lives.

> The mindset of debt needs to be dealt with before you get out of debt.

For the record, mortgages are good, when they are good, when the interest is in a healthy place, and you have a plan to get out of the mortgage. The sooner you pay off your home, the less you end up paying for it.

STREETS OF GOLD

We end up in debt so often when we try and buy things that we don't need and at the end of day don't matter. I think the best way to end this chapter is with a joke my mom once told, and I'm 100% sure she stole it.

There once was a businessman who had incredible wealth beyond any comparison. He had everything he could ever want. He bought many things to fill up his home, but one day out of nowhere he was hit by a bus.

The man gets up to heaven and goes up to Jesus and is disappointed. Jesus looks at the man and says, "Why are you upset?" The man looks at Jesus with tears in his eyes and replies, "I just wish I could have brought some of my things with me." Jesus decides to let this man do just that, so he sends him back to earth for one day to get anything he desires, but it must fit in one suitcase. I don't know why, but Jesus is in charge so you follow the rules.

The man goes back to earth and in one day sells all of his possessions and then takes all of that money and all of his investments and savings (this guy had goals, just saying…), all of his wealth, and traded it in for as many gold bars as he could fill in the suitcase.

GRAPE JELLY

After he filled the suitcase with gold bars, he was taken back to heaven where he once again met with Jesus. Jesus was curious what the man decided to bring. With excitement and joy in his eyes, the man opened the suitcase. Jesus laughed and said, "You brought pavement?"

The moral of the story is that we end up working hard and can get into debt for temporary things. Let's not strive for pavement. Let's strive to have a life that truly makes a difference to others.

LEAVING EGYPT

When I read about the Israelites in the desert, I find it fascinating, because it's so similar to the way people deal with finances. You are a slave to the lender so when we're leaving Egypt we are leaving slavery and the same when you are leaving debt.Faith was leaving Egypt. Wisdom was going to the pharaoh asking to leave. If they would've just left, they would've died. God gave them the wisdom to ask.

Some of you are faithful, and some of you are stupid faithful. Just because you pray for it doesn't mean God will give it to you. Just because you want to win the lottery doesn't mean that you're going to. For many of you, the lottery would destroy you. If you see the way you handle little, what damage would you do with much? The same is true with faith.

If you got into debt, it's on you to pay it off. I paid off my student debt, and I don't want to be forced into paying anyone else's. **The Bible talks about giving to the poor and needy, but it says nothing about helping out the lazy.** If you have student debt, or any consumer debt, it's your responsibly to take over.

MY $40,000 PROBLEM

I'm not a huge fan of resolutions, I never have been. They just seem to rarely work out. In the first week of January of 2020, I was praying about a couple of random things to be honest.

We don't talk to God about what we think we should talk to God about. We talk to God about what we actually want to talk to God about.

So, I was talking to God about some movies that were coming out and some random date ideas I had for my wife, and I then out of nowhere (for me this is a good sign that God was speaking to me) my student debt came to mind: $40,000. I was thinking about that number for a second. I was thinking about how massive it felt, how every month we were paying $500 towards something from years ago. That is enough to hate debt. The fact that many people are paying off meals, cars, schooling, and vacations that are just memories feels wrong. I was thinking about that $40,000, and then it came to my mind that we made more than $40,000 combined in the last year and are on track to make even more in the next year. We've been having this happen. We have made more money year after year ever since we've been married. Granted, in our first year we had a combined income of whatever an ice cream store makes in the month of December. But it still counts and is one of our favorite parts of our financial story.

I did the math the quickly and realized that if we moved some things around, we could stop living as if we didn't have debt. We could hustle to make more income on top of what we were making now. I believed that if we focused not on just making more money, but making more of our money, that we could win. It seemed like a reality that becoming debt free could be on the horizon for us. All it took was breaking things down to figure out how to make more. After talking with my wife, she was all in, instantly.

OUR PLAN TO PAY OF $40,000 IN 12 MONTHS

1. ROUNDING UP
We rounded up our debt to the nearest thousand: **$40,000** (for easy math). We technically owed $39,752.18, but that isn't easy to divide by, and we needed this to be simple for us, so that this process was simple as it really is.

2. FIGURE OUT A MONTHLY GOAL
Divide it by 12 months since that was our goal to be debt free in that one year. **That equaled $3,333 a month.** If you think that's a ton of money, that would be the correct feeling that you should have. Hold on though.

3. SUBTRACT THE MINIMUM

Take $3,333 and subtract the current monthly payment of $500. **That equals $2,833 left a month.** This is the amount that had to be paid no matter what. It helped us feel as though we already were starting below the monthly goal that was already in the budget.

4. NUDGE THE BUDGET

We then look at our budget and lived a different lifestyle or found places where we could trim our budget. We were able to pay an additional $1,700 each month because of that. This is when it became essential to have side hustles and multiple streams of income. In our home we made CONSISTENT INCOME from a salary and a graphic design business. This is what we lived off of. Our INCONSISTENT INCOME was speaking engagements, book sales, and occasional miscellaneous hustles. We say that it's not consistent, because some months, for example, we speak 4 times, and other months it may only be once, so we budget based on consistency. That's just to give some perspective. **That equaled $1,133 left a month.** I understand that not everyone can find $1,700 a month in their current budget, which was true for us. We weren't just going on vacations every month. This was us trimming every single budget to needs-based spending only. This was us not putting anything (only for one year) additional into investing for our future/retirement, no vacations, and eating out only when it financially made sense (which is almost never). We cut every other area you can think of. We pushed t to the limit.

5. WHY DIDN'T WE DO THIS BEFORE?

We then came to the realization that another thing we could do is rent out a room in our house. As I write this book, we currently have no children, and our house has the ability to do so. We were able to get a tenet who would pay $500 a month in rent. **That equaled $633 left a month.** At this point, we could see how possible this was becoming. Also in this time, because of our home being a part of an HOA, I was asked to be the president of it at the same time, which I found out gave me the benefit of not having to pay my HOA fee which was $93 a month. This all equaled $540 a month that we have left to figure out.

6. WHAT IS LEFT (HUSTLE)

In order to make our goal of getting out of debt in one year, we had to come up with **$540 left a month** outside of our consistent income. We also had to be prepared to have other expenses that could happen (which is why we had savings and emergency funds). This meant that any books sales, speaking engagements, new clients, bonuses, and raises would 100% go toward our goal of getting out of debt in 2020. An increase in income should increase your outcome, so we set aside raises before we got them.

Granted, this all only works if nothing unexpected comes up and doesn't wipe out your emergency fund. However, because we had gotten advice long before this process, we had a little over $7,000 in savings in case of emergencies. We got to this because of the chapter

"Savings is a Piece of Cake." That number is strategic as it broke down our finances to two months of expenses if we both lost every single amount of income (unlikely). We planned for the unlikely, so we could live unlike anyone else.

THE OUTCOME

I get that some reading this story could be led to frustration. It's hard to read about other people's freedom when you're still in consumer debt. You can get out of it. I know you can. **The only reason you're still in debt is because you are too comfortable not having multiple jobs.** If you could be miserable for one year, it would make the rest of your years incredible. I know this because we did this.

At the end of this process, at the end of your process of getting out debt, you want to s otherwise, you'll get back into debt. The goal isn't just to be out of debt, but into a better and healthier financial place. We got real about getting out of debt, because we heard from God, but also because we have plans for our future that require faith. In total honesty, it's harder to have faith when you also have chains. Removing the chains and slavery of debt freed us up to do whatever God had planned for us. God has a plan for you that you can't even currently dream about. Getting out of debt might make that picture come into more reality for you.

Reflection

ARE YOU CURRENTLY TRYING TO KILL DEBTS THAT ARE COSTING YOU MORE THAN THEY'RE MAKING YOU? (YOUR ANSWER BETTER BE YES...)

WHAT IS SOMETHING YOU'RE LOOKING FORWARD TO ONCE YOUR BAD DEBTS ARE GONE?

Broke

If you don't have your money all together, that's alright (for now). You're simply at a starting place, and we all start somewhere. This must mean that you'll have a better story to tell later. You may even say that you're broke, but being broke isn't the same as being broken. **We don't need to identify with our money issues. We just need to identify our money issues.**

In college, I did freelance graphic design, and I was making really good money for a Bible college student. What that means is that I made less than $1,000 a month, but it was more than everyone else around me. I would regularly want to go out to eat, see a movie, and do what I wanted to do. I would often want to do it with others. The response was almost always, "I'm broke. I'm poor."

GRAPE JELLY

I wish they would've just said, "I can't right now."

Too often, we tell ourselves, others, and even kids, "No, we can't." We need to transition that to, "No we can't right now, **but someday.**" What this does is it shifts our minds from the current problem to the future solution.

QUALIFY YOUR SOMEDAY

In college, I had a friend who told me a quote that I'm sure he didn't make up. We went out to lunch, had a great time, and I told him, "We need to hang out again someday." He responded with something I have never forgotten. He told me, "Someday never happens." What is wild is that was the last time we ever had a meal together. We never hung out again. Why? Because I never qualified what someday meant. I never actually took action steps, because the action was never defined.

Many of you are in broken financial systems, because you keep "some-day-ing" yourself out of actual solutions. "When are you going to do that dream you told me about? When are you going to start that business?" If the response you have to your dreams is "someday," your dream will likely never happen, because someday never happens.

You need to give qualifiers to what makes a day a someday. What this really is, is a risk assessment. The easiest way to qualify what makes a someday is by doing a simple breakdown of what are the worst and best case scenarios.

Let's go with the idea that maybe as you read this you hate your occupation. You've been in it for a while, given it a chance, but maybe it hasn't seemed to give you a chance. You are ready to get out, and you have a dream of moving on. Let's worst and best case this...

Worst case scenario: you get another crappy job. Best case: everything works out better than you dreamed. The more you start making comparisons like this, you'll soon realize that your worst case scenario isn't that bad, or you may realize that you are already in your worst case, so you have nothing to lose. Too many of us are living in our Plan-B instead of God's Plan-A.

My belief for you reading this is that you need to move from, *"What if it doesn't work out,"* to *"What if everything works out better than I think it could."* **One of those is Grape Jelly. The other is prosperity.**

"RICH" IS FOR POOR PEOPLE

At the same time, I understand the hardship of wanting for more than you've had. It's a massive hurdle of our thoughts, family of origin, and the stories we tell ourselves.

Growing up I would ride the school bus for what felt like an eternity (20 minutes, but still). I listened to some music and would drive through the "rich people's neighborhood." It was labeled this by my family, as we would drive by. Even though it was never fully stated, it was passively implied that a place like that, a neighborhood like that, wouldn't be for us. In reality, the size of your home doesn't matter, but **when you put a ceiling on dreams, you'll always end up staring at them.**

Rich is a term often used by those who are poor. Rich has no variables, no real definition, and no measurement. Rich is the ambiguous word that we use to excuse our own lack. That's why I believe rich is for poor people. The double meaning is that if you want to be rich, you can be, if you make it happen. At the same time, it's also a poor person's concept. Don't strive to be rich. Strive to reach a thought-out goal. Find a someday, qualify it, and then reach it. I'd rather reach my somedays than anyone else's rich days.

BANKRUPT YOUR BELIEF SYSTEM

If you're reading this, there's a good chance that your past or even current situation is one of financial failure. I know this, because you're human. Financial failure isn't final. It's a teacher. **Financial failure fuels future fortune.** If you get hold of what's been holding you back, you can reposition yourself to greater prosperity and live the life you're called to.

God isn't calling you to be a millionaire, He is calling you to live better. **You're called to live under your means and above your mentalities.** We all go through difficult times, and yet in those moments, our relationship with God has the greatest opportunity to grow. **Even when I'm not fruitful, God is still faithful.**

IT'S OKAY

There is something that I believe deeply. It's okay to not be okay; but you just can't stay there forever. If you're broke and out of money right now, it's okay to be bummed about it for a day. After that day though, get up, clean yourself up, and find a way to hustle your way back to where you need to be. When we got out of debt aggressively, in order to get to our free goal for ourselves and money, I had a total of five jobs at the time. We fig ured our way out of debt. We found ourselves out of a broken system through God's wisdom and our human hustle.

On the other side of things, some-
times what's broken about us isn't just that things aren't okay, but many of us have a problem when things are okay. Maybe it's just me **Even when I'm not fruitful, God is still faithful.**
(I know that's not true, but it helps us feel better right?), but I have this feeling when things are going very well in money, marriage, family, and business. I find a way to not enjoy it. I grape jelly myself into fearing that it won't last, so why enjoy it now? I want to give you permission for something I'm continually working on. It's okay to not be okay. It's also okay to be okay. I want to give you the freedom to enjoy the moments when things are go-

133

ing well. Use the mountain top moments of life to enjoy the view instead of worrying about what would happen if you fall.

Far too many of us are broken when things are good or bad, which tells us something. The times don't dictate how I am. I dictate how I am. It's okay to not be okay, but it's also okay to be okay.

Reflection

WHAT DO YOU THINK IS THE MOST BROKEN PART ABOUT YOUR MONEY SYSTEM?

WHAT DO YOU THINK GOD WANTS TO DO WITH THAT PART OF YOU?

GRAPE JELLY

First Class Life

You are called to a first-class life. I believe that for you with my entire faith and belief system. Grape jelly might have been a part of you, but my prayer is that it becomes apart from you. It's time for you to get an upgrade. A first-class life is one where you may be going to the same destination as others around you, but the trip to the destination is a higher-level experience.

I have learned that often times it's hard to believe without seeing first. Let's be real. Faith is difficult at first. God is going to show what is possible through others. This is a major twist from often comparing yourself to others, a problem that many of us have. I used to get frustrated growing up flying on planes and would walk past first class, past business, past coach, until we had our seats right in front of the toilet. I felt judged, and it felt like first class was a different, unattainable world.

When I was in high school, my family of origin adopted two kids from Haiti, and due to some wild and crazy last-minute changes due to an earthquake, we were told to get on a plane as soon as possible to pick them up. My family couldn't find any tickets anywhere, and we had to get to the other side of the country. After some bizarre conversations, my mom ended up telling me and my sister that we were driving to get on a private jet to get our brother and sister.

> God is going to show what is possible through others.

This wasn't just any private jet. It was an executive private jet for a fortune 500 company. Som there I am with my family. We couldn't have felt more out of place. I was wearing a fake luxury watch and was just soaking it all in.

We got to Florida where our new siblings had just landed, and we became a larger family overnight. We stayed a few days in Florida, having some new family time, and then got ready to fly back home. The private jet wasn't waiting for us. We flew back on a budget airline in the last seats right in front of the bathroom. From a multi-million dollar executive jets to $56 super saver toilet seats.

After that moment, I would try as much as possible, like

any teenager would, to bring up that I flew private.

It wouldn't be for at least a solid decade before I got anywhere closer to first class. Now I fly constantly and am upgraded on almost every single flight. It might not be private, but I'll take first class any day. I am upgraded for a very specific reason. I'm faithful to a single airline. I will pay more for a flight to stay faithful. **Your faithfulness has benefits.**

I DON'T FISH

I have never successfully fished a day in my life. I never plan to fish again in my life if I'm honest. I have this fear that I will get a fish hook stuck on me. This is also why I've never done drugs. I don't want to get hooked. (That joke is funny, just go with it).

However, there is someone in the Bible who was a professional fisherman, and who traded his profession for a promise of a first-class life. There's this guy named Peter, and by the end of his life, he was one of the early leaders of the church at large. Before that, he would walk in the streets, and his shadow would touch someone, and they would be healed. Before that, he walked on water. Before that, he saw miracles. But before any of what was just listed, he was a fisherman in Capernaum, a blue-collar fishing town where no one dreamed of living. Yet Jesus met with Peter in this place...

On one occasion, while the crowd was pressing in on him

*to hear the word of God, he was standing by the lake of Gennesaret, and he saw two boats by the lake, but the fishermen had gone out of them and were washing their nets. Getting into one of the boats, which was Simon's, he asked him to put out a little from the land. And he sat down and taught the people from the boat. And when he had finished speaking, he said to Simon, "Put out into the deep and let down your nets for a catch." And Simon answered, "Master, we toiled all night and took nothing! But at your word I will drop the net" And when they had done this, they enclosed a large number of fish, and their nets were breaking. They signaled to their partners in the other boat to come and help them. And they came and filled both the boats, so that they began to sink. But when Simon Peter saw it, he fell down at Jesus' knees, saying, "Depart from me, for I am a sinful man, O Lord." For he and all who were with him were astonished at the catch of fish that they had taken, 10 and so also were James and John, sons of Zebedee, who were partners with Si-mon. And Jesus said to Simon, "Do not be afraid; from now on you will be catching men."**And when they had brought their boats to land, they left everything and followed him.***
LUKE 5:2-11

There are a lot of wild moments in this historical narrative written in the book of Luke. One thing that I learned about fishing, even though I never do it, is that back when this happened, and where it happened, they would've fished in a very specific way. Peter would've been fishing in the shallows in the evening when and where the water would be warmest. That's how fishing was done then.

However, Jesus doesn't just tell Peter go and fish again in the right way of doing it. Jesus tells Peter to go in the deep during the day. This doesn't make any sense to a fisherman. This is the worst idea possible. But what we find out is that **Jesus' worst is better than my best.**

This miracle moment is one of provision, income, and prosperity that Jesus has with Peter. Yet, there was something better that was to come for Peter. Peter had the opportunity to cash out and take advantage of the situation, but instead leaves all of it to follow Jesus. Following Jesus is worth any monetary sacrifice. Let's be honest, what a better story, catching the most fish you've ever caught to make a lot of money, or seeing Jesus multiple fish to feed thousands?

I used to wonder though, why was Jesus in Capernaum? He should've been in Jerusalem where the spiritual elite were. Jesus was in Capernaum, this smelly blue collar fishing town, to let everyone know, that what Jesus has, is for everyone.

I believe blue collar workers can have white collar callings. You might keep your job but find a new calling within it that makes it white collar, clean, and more meaningful.

FLY WITH OTHERS

GRAPE JELLY

The more I've been upgraded when flying, the more I've realized how much nicer people are when you're in first class.

I love this story of Peter catching more fish, because part of the blessing, a reason why there were two boats full of fish, is because Peter invited others into his provision. Peter was overwhelmed with the abundance, so much so it was breaking his nets. He called to his friends in the other boat to help him, and boats both were filled.

There is something about being Peter and having the faith to go into deep waters and do something that doesn't make sense to you, only to find out that it's better than your best plan. At the same time, it's just as crazy to be invited into it even when you had nothing to do with the obedience that led to the blessing.

First class can be fun, but it's more fun when someone is with you. My wife doesn't fly even close to as much as I do, yet when she flies with me, she gets upgraded. She benefits from my faithfulness in the airline. So, here's the question. Do others benefit from your faithfulness? This is what shows others if you're a good friend. Then on the other side of this, do you benefit from their faithfulness? This is what shows you if you have good friends.

GIVING AWAY FIRST CLASS

I grew up thinking that first class on a plane would never happen for me. It was always out of reach. I thought having nice things was out of reach. Now, I get upgraded to first class constantly because of how often I fly. If I'm really honest, it no longer matters. The first couple times I would take photos, send them to my wife or post them, but because it happens constantly now, I don't feel it anymore. If anything, I often give it away. If I see someone who has an infant in his or her arms, meaning that he or she will have to sit with the baby on a lap the entire flight, I will almost always give my seat away to that person. I do this for two main reasons. The first is because I have a kid, and know what it's like to fly with a baby. Secondly, and way more fun, is that I like to see the faces of the old business people when they see a screaming baby that's about to sit next to them for the next few hours. Maybe it's messed up, but nothing brings me more joy.

My belief, prayer, and hope for you is that you don't just get occasional first-class upgrades in your life, but that it would be so often that you're able to give those moments to others. I like flying first class, but it's way more fun to see someone sit there, who might never be able to outside of me giving it to them.

DROP THE PARACHUTE

Peter dropped a fishing net when it made no sense. He didn't just drop a fishing net. He left his safety net. Pilots never wear parachutes, yet we walk around wearing them, just in case God doesn't catch us. God doesn't need to catch us. We need to catch up. We need to catch up with God has already called us to.

God is calling you to drop your net, to get rid of the parachute, and to follow him.

I told a story in this book about when I left a job doing graphic design to fully follow the call of God on my life. Graphic design had always been my backup plan. My plan b. My net. My parachute. In case God didn't show up, I always could take care of myself. I used to brag about how I would take care of myself, but my brag was the most broken part about me.

Drop the net, leave the parachute at home, rip up plan B, and follow God's plan A for your life. It's a first-class life.

Reflection

LET'S SAY YOU COULD WRITE DOWN YOUR FIRST-CLASS LIFE, AND IT WOULD COME REAL. WHAT WOULD IT LOOK LIKE?

DO YOU STRUGGLE TAKING A NICER SEAT WHEN YOU'VE NEVER HAD ONE BEFORE, OR ARE YOU QUICK TO HAVE A SEAT?

WHAT PARACHUTE OR PLAN B DO YOU NEED TO LET GO OF?

GRAPE JELLY

Confession

I still eat grape jelly sandwiches on occasion. There, I said it. I wrote this whole book about how bad grape jelly is both in your sandwich and your mindset, yet I still have grape jelly.

I get my savings messed up. I can overspend, and I always go over budget for any occasion where gifts are given. Health with our faith and money can be sweet, but it is also sticky. It's hard to move forward from our past. It took me a lot of coaching, therapy, and hustle to get from the little kid who wanted roller skate shoes, to now being okay when things aren't okay. I am not my finances.

Money is a tool that God wants to empower you with

if you can handle it. God wants to give good gifts to his kids. There's no guilt in asking God for more when He has an unlimited amount of it. How funny is it that we can stress out in our grape jelly thoughts, thinking God will be frustrated if we ask for more when His driveway and sidewalk is made of gold. We work so hard to get gold when He walks on it.

I remember for years thinking how incredible it was that I hadn't had a boss since I was 18 years old. I started this book out with this story. Let's wrap it with the same. For the longest time, years, if not almost decades, I would continually think about how good life was, because I had made my success by myself. By myself meant in terms of that I didn't have a boss, I had no backup, it was just me doing my own thing, being my own boss.

I would brag about this. For the longest time, I didn't understand how you could be happy if you had a boss, if you worked a normal work week, or did what you didn't love. In so many ways, I thought my life was better than many, because I wasn't chained to the same lifestyle. Then, I realized that many people love the security of a salary. They like being on a team. They like knowing that they have backup, and it's not all riding on them. I would laugh at this thinking that my life was incredible, because I had no one else to take credit for my achievements. I would brag on this. But one day when I was getting some coaching, I realized that most of my desires are about what everyone else has. I realized that I wanted to brag about doing things by myself when I needed

148

to learn to lean on others. I was bragging about the part of me that was most broken.

POVERTY MENTALITY

Grape jelly is our synonym for having a poverty mentality. Such mentalities exist in two main forms: people who hoard their money in fear that it will go away, or those who spend it quickly in fear that it won't be there the next time they look for it.

HOW TO BREAK THE GRAPE JELLY JAR

I'm a big proponent of equality of thought, especially with finances. Many of us have a worst-case scenario in our mind when it comes to our money. If you're going to think of the absolute worst, not that you should, you need to at the least for balance sake, think of the best case scenario as well. When is the last time you sat and thought about what the best outcome could be for your finances? If I did this God's way, what would my financial health look like? The best way to get out of grape jelly is to shop for other jelly. You need faith for the future for something better than the worst-case scenario of getting your needs met.

The best way to beat a poverty mentality is to have greater faith in your future while having the wisdom to work hard for that future. A way to exercise your faith with your finances is through generosity. Giving will break your poverty and the mentality that holds onto you.

GRAPE JELLY

If we're honest with ourselves, a grape jelly lifestyle, a "I don't deserve that," attitude is often derived from a part of us being broken on the inside. Where your treasure is your heart will be. That's real. I also believe that where your hurt is your wallet will be too. We often try to over control in areas, in which we have the most fear. What would it look like if you stopped thinking the worst and had faith in the best? Had faith in what God says about tithing and giving?

Tithing is the key that unlocks provision for you. Giving is the key that unlocks the chains of poverty from you.

Reflection

WHAT IS AN AREA IN YOUR LIFE, IN WHICH YOU WANT TO BREAK THE GRAPE JELLY JAR?

WHAT'S THE NEXT STEP FOR YOU IN YOUR JOURNEY AWAY FROM GRAPE JELLY?

GRAPE JELLY

About the Author

Ty Buckingham is inordinately passionate about helping people make the complicated simple and the awkward not. For years he has traveled around the world, preaching and teaching.

Married to Rebecca, they currently reside outside of Atlanta, GA with their son Moses.

TYBUCKINGHAM.COM

www.ingramcontent.com/pod-product-compliance
Lightning Source LLC
Chambersburg PA
CBHW072144090426
42739CB00013B/3275